DANCING
IN THE
DARK

DANCING
IN THE
DARK

A Sister Grieves

Elsie K. Neufeld

Foreword by David Augsburger

HERALD PRESS
Waterloo, Ontario
Scottdale, Pennsylvania

Canadian Cataloguing in Publication Data
Neufeld, Elsie K., 1957-
   Dancing in the dark

Includes bibliographical references.
ISBN 0-8361-3537-7

1. Klassen, John Victor, d. 1987—Death and burial.   2. Neufeld,
Elsie K., 1957-   .   3. Bereavement—Psychological aspects.
4. Grief.   5. Brothers and sisters—Death—Psychological
aspects. 6. Death—Religious aspects—Mennonite.   I. Title.

BF575.G7N48   1990   155.9'37   C90-095258-X

The paper used in this publication is recycled and meets the minimum
requirements of American National Standard for Information
Sciences—Permanence of Paper for Printed Library Materials,
ANSI Z39.48-1984.

To my parents:
For their
model of courage
and faith

My three children—
Daniel, Matthew, and Rachel:
Their presence and many recollections
have shaped this story

The "forgotten mourners":
all who have lost an adult sibling.
We are not alone.

Contents

New Pathways

Foreword

Loss connects.

Connection brings support, release, renewal of hope.

Hope springs from grace experienced.

Grace experienced, even in times of intense loss, needs embodiment. It must have a human face.

The face of grace is marked by pain, gentled by grief; its power comes from wounds healed.

Wound and healing reflect and express the central archetype of life—the God who came among us as a wounded healer—the risen Christ.

This chain of linking insights runs throughout *Dancing in the Dark,* revealing the intimate relationship between our suffering and the one who suffers with us.

After learning that my friend Elsie Neufeld was writing a manuscript, I asked for the privilege of reading the first draft. Then I wrote,

Dear Elsie:
  I read the book immediately.
  I was deeply, deeply moved. Having grieved much during the last two years, I found myself participating in your grief, loss, and pain at a level I didn't want to express, just experience; I had to lay it aside and live with it awhile. The privilege of walking alongside another sufferer is nourishing, healing. It is being joined by a cotraveler through pain.
  It's a story of deep integrity. It must be told. . . .

Now, as this book is released, the story of a sister's grief over the tragic loss of a brother can serve as a mirror for our own coping with crisis and pain.

Dancing in the Dark lets you share a stormy voyage across inner seas to a new resolution and the discovery of reconciliation. It illuminates the grieving process so that the pathways of healing where we grope in the dark become a little safer. Along the way we learn the crucial lessons about grief and loss. We learn that

—grieving is spiral, repetitive, cyclical, not linear and logically progressive. We return to our loss again and again, yet each time another part of injury is cleansed, knit together, sealed again.

—grieving is disorderly, not arranged in tidy stages. It invades our thoughts and feelings in sudden, unpredictable, uncontrollable ways. It overwhelms our hopes to be moderate, organized, in control of our feelings.

—grieving is insensitive to time, intolerant of our schedules. The past remains with us, the future loses its meaning, the present feels stuck and frozen while others seem to rush ahead.

—grieving is not forgetting but slowly transforming the loss into a renewed capacity to live with both loss and discovery.

—grieving never fully ends. To grieve properly is not to forget, exclude, escape the loss entirely. It is to let go of the pain, let the future come again, and let oneself be present with life and others here and now.

—grieving is not the end of life. It is the beginning of a deeper understanding of life's meaning, welded from the fragments and shards of our brokenness into a beauty that is enhanced by darkness and light, shadow and brightness, suffering and joy.

In grief, one feels deeply that the heart will never dance again . . . but healing holds surprises.

—*David Augsburger*

Acknowledgments

Special thanks to

Murray Phillips, who accompanied me through the highs and lows of this book. Without him, this book would not have come to life. Not only did you graciously correct my grammar and punctuation, you also encouraged, affirmed, and connected me with the right publisher. I am forever indebted.

Marie Riediger, who gave me mourner status and pointed me toward, and then accompanied me to, the land of healing. You were God's arms around me.

Betty and *Jim McMichael*—to Betty for telling me about the Grief Recovery program and to Jim for your presence at the trial. It meant a lot.

David Augsburger, for asking to read the manuscript, for affirming the value of the story, and finally, for celebrating its acceptance for publication with Herald Press.

Katie Funk Wiebe, for affirming and encouraging the writer in me. You've become my role model.

Walter, my husband, and our children, *Daniel, Matthew,* and *Rachel*. Without your cooperation this book would not have been completed. Thanks for all the times you left the house and ate at McDonald's so I could have some quiet "computer time." I love you more than words can say.

Walter and *Susanna Klassen*, my parents; *Katie Neufeld*, my mother-in-law; and my friend *Evita*. Thanks for your consistent help with the children. That has been a gift.

My friends, who were brave enough to ask about the book and braver still to read it. You know who you are.

Michael King, my editor. Not only were you a most understanding editor, you've also become a friend. I cherish that.

Periodicals which have printed material related to this book, including *The Mennonite, Mennonite Brethren Herald, Mennonite Reporter*, and *Purpose*.

God, my author, for leading me to the land of words, then directing my mind and pen to attempt to articulate this journey. Never before have I felt your presence so near. I am eternally grateful.

Introduction

The death of a parent, I've often read, severs you from your past; the death of a spouse, from your present; and the death of a child, from your future. Then does the death of an adult sibling sever you from all three? I think so.

An adult sibling is part of your past and your present. You expect him or her to be part of your future as well. In that sense, the death of a sibling can be the most difficult loss of all.

Siblings are part of your whole life. You expect parents to die because they're older. A spouse doesn't usually enter your life until adulthood. And your children, though borne by you, are also part of your adult life. But a sibling—a brother like John—is special. A sibling is a gift.

For a long time I wondered why John's death affected me so profoundly, why my grief was so intense. He was, after all, "just" my brother.

These words from Marie, a grief counselor, finally released me. "Yes," she said, looking me straight in the eyes, "but he was *your* brother."

She was right. He was *my* brother. He was *my* friend. I deserved and claimed my right to grieve as intensely as I needed. John was my past, my present, my future.

George Santayana said "One's friends are that part of the human race with which one can be human." That is what John was to me, someone I could be human with. When John came he didn't judge my housecleaning, cooking, or appearance. He simply came to be with me and my family.

Shortly after the first anniversary of John's death, I

13

visited his grave. I placed a big bunch of wildflowers by his tombstone, then sat on the grass beside it. "A brother will always be a brother, but if you're really lucky, he'll also be your friend," I said. I was very lucky; John was my friend.

■ ■ ■

I'm an avid reader. People tease me because I have a book to recommend for every circumstance. But I believe in "bibliotherapy"—so after John's death it was natural for me to look for books about grief and mourning. I especially searched for one dealing with the death of an adult sibling. I found dozens of books on the grief process. Only one focused on the death of a sibling. Even this one didn't meet my needs. It dealt strictly with the loss, not the life that had preceded. I would have to write my own book.

"It's too bad your children won't remember their uncle John," my father said one day.

I was shocked. "Of course they'll remember. They loved him; they're old enough to remember."

My father shook his head. "It won't be the same. What will they remember?"

And so this book was born. I had to write it, if only so my children could remember. Slowly, slowly the pages filled. I was surprised how much I had forgotten until I took the time to remember.

The memories flooded back. That was the easy part. But I wasn't prepared for the chronic self-doubt which accompanied me as I wrote.

"It doesn't matter if your reasons change as you go along. Don't get discouraged, keep writing," my husband said after one such slump.

He was right. Perhaps it was good that my reasons kept changing, because the longer I wrote the more reasons I found to finish. Each doubt I faced was countered by another reason to continue.

The more I talk with others about their experiences of death and loss, the more I know there are no easy answers to the questions crises stir. Nor are there quick recipes for getting better.

Death and grief are horrible. They are lonely, painful experiences no one can fully understand without personally walking through them.

I hope this book can help prepare those who have never experienced a significant loss for what they, too, will someday face. I also hope this book can offer a doorway into the lives of people like myself who have experienced a death. Not having experienced a death is no excuse to avoid those who have.

"It is ironic that we who have suffered and need comforting most must be the ones to teach others how to comfort us," someone said to me recently. People *can* learn how to respond, if they want to. I hope this book can help those who sincerely want to be comforters.

Recently I heard someone tell a person in mourning that "eventually you've got to stop bleeding. Otherwise, you might as well lie down in the grave beside the one who's died."

I do want to stop bleeding. I want to air the wound John's death has caused inside of me. No longer do I want to hide my pain; I want a proper healing, not a slick, bandaged recovery. And I want to deal with my feelings about God's will. Did God cause my brother's death? Or is God helping me face his death?

This book had to be finished, primarily for me, I think. It was my audible grief. It was my goodbye to John, my farewell to a brother who will always be loved, always remembered. Now it's time to let go, to face life again, with eyes and ears and mouth and hands and mind and feelings washed clean by the thousands of tears I have shed over the death of my brother John.

On the first anniversary of John's death I placed a notice in our local newspaper. "John—in death you are more present than in life." This paradox is true. John is gone but he is still here.

I find great comfort in these words.

> *And when the stream*
> *Which overflowed the soul was passed away,*
> *A consciousness remained that it had left,*
> *Deposited upon the silent shore*
> *of memory, images and precious thought*
> *That shall not die, and cannot be destroyed.*
> —Wordsworth

Before I proceed I must introduce my family, for they helped shape this story. My husband was John's close friend long before Walter and I married. The additional role of brother-in-law only deepened an already close relationship.

Daniel, now eight, has also greatly influenced my memories. He repeatedly asks the big "why" questions. "Why did Uncle John have to die? Why can't he come back?" I hope someday this book will help him change his questions.

Matthew, now six, is our eternal optimist. He assures us that Uncle John is in heaven, that he has a new body, and that he is living in Matthew's heart. Matthew's logic is simple and clear: Uncle John is alive. Matthew sends him messages via balloons.

Rachel, our youngest child, denied a relationship with her uncle John, the pilot, is a living pointer to life. Already at age one, she noticed every airplane flying overhead.

"She's copying you," a friend told me.

"No," I replied, "I never taught her that."

Today, at age two, she not only lifts her eyes to the sky at the mere sound of airplanes, she also points and yells enthusiastically, "Airplane, airplane!" It leaves me wondering . . . perhaps she met her uncle John in passing?

I'm grateful for my family. They were my lifeline when I couldn't face another day without John. They've been my living photograph of hope.

On March 16, 1987, I picked up *The News*, our local newspaper. This was on the front page.

Driver Killed in Crash and Fire

An Abbotsford man was killed Sunday night in a two-vehicle accident and resulting fire on Highway 11 north of Huntingdon.

Dead is 32-year-old John Victor Klassen, driver of a southbound Volkswagen "beetle." It burst into flames on impact, said RCMP.

Abbotsford RCMP said the accident occurred at about 10 p.m., approximately 300 feet north of the intersection of Vye Road and Highway 11.

A northbound 1978 Dodge passenger car driven by Joseph Dixon, 31, of Abbotsford, attempted to pass a vehicle which had turned onto Highway 11 from Vye Road.

The vehicle driven by Dixon collided head-on with the southbound car, said Abbotsford RCMP.

RCMP said investigation is continuing.

Klassen was co-owner of Airspread, a crop-dusting firm based in Chilliwack.

"Klassen" was my brother, older by two years.

This book records my journey following the news John was dead, through the void John left, through the pain of learning that the driver of the other car was drunk, and through the challenge of living again after experiencing such horror.

This book is written from my perspective, my recollections. It's not my aim to interpret John or make him something he was not. I'm simply recording my journey.

I have changed some names to protect identities. If by including or excluding certain events and people I offend anyone, I apologize in advance.

MOURNING APPAREL

What shall I wear to show the world
how much I miss you?
Shall I wear frowns and tears and downcast faces
never looking up from your now-buried self?
Shall I wear black to mirror back for all the world to
  see
the void your death has left?
Or shall I wear rainbow-colored clothing
to point to life, as your forever-silenced body does?
Shall I lift my face and put on upturned, rosy lipstick
or shall I be true, and laugh and weep
and sing and wail together?
My face a mask
once this, once that.
A furrowed brow turned upside-down
becomes a smile;
a smiling mouth turned right-side-up
becomes a frown.
What shall I do now, brother John?
Tell me, please,
or are you sleeping?
Brother John? Brother John?
Mourning bells are ringing,
mourning bells are ringing
Ding Dong Ding,
Ding! Dong! Ding!

Death:
The Original Sin

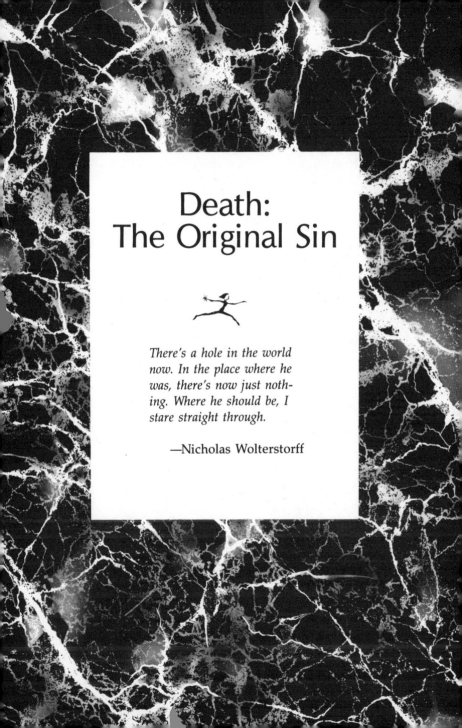

There's a hole in the world now. In the place where he was, there's now just nothing. Where he should be, I stare straight through.

—Nicholas Wolterstorff

1
Death Visits

The day before Good Friday. The day before the anniversary of Christ's death. An appropriate day to write about John's last day on earth.

Unlike Christ on his last day, John didn't know it was to be his last. Although I wonder—did he know subconsciously?

I don't know all he did and thought and felt that day. But I can say what I saw and did and felt, and what others observed and later told me.

It was a Sunday, an ordinary, sunny, nearly spring Sunday. John had arrived home from Winnipeg the previous evening and spent the night in Chilliwack (twenty miles away), where he had landed his plane. It had been a business trip—to investigate buying another spray plane. Unfortunately, it hadn't been successful.

Now home, he called us.

After a short conversation about his trip, I told him we would drop off his car later, on our way to Walt's mom. "Can you wait that long?" I asked.

"Yes," he said.

"Guess what, guys!" I told the boys, "Uncle John is back and needs his car again."

"Oh, no! That means we won't have a car again," Daniel said. Matthew shouted, "Hurrah, he's back," and searched through his preschool drawings for one to take to Uncle John.

John was just coming out of his house when we drove up. Walt was already outside, talking to John, when I left the car. I was seven months pregnant and moving slowly.

The strangest, most insignificant things stay frozen in my mind. I wore a pink maternity dress. I had just had my shoulder-length hair cut short a few days before.

"Your wife got her hair cut—looks good," I heard John say to Walt as I approached. He grinned at me.

"Welcome back," I said.

"Here Uncle John, this is for you," said Matthew. He handed John a black, paper leprechaun hat with green shamrocks glued on it.

"Hey, nice, Matthew. St. Patrick's Day, eh? Thanks a lot," Uncle John responded.

What did we talk about in that last conversation? I don't remember much. It wasn't a long talk. I know we talked again of his trip to Manitoba, about how cold and ugly "Windypeg" was. But most of all, I remember his commenting on the green grass, the budding trees, the "daffs."

"Yup," he said, on the intake of breath, then broke into his renowned "hyena" laugh.

He apologized for having to take back his car, knowing that left me without a vehicle during the week. "I'm going to have my motorcycle insured soon. Then you can use my car again," he told me apologetically.

"It's okay, I don't mind walking."

He and Walt went off to check out his motorcycle—a

new Kawasaki 750. I stood watching from the distance, watching as they exchanged that casual bantering back and forth of words, which almost always meant more than they actually said. The two had an easygoing, almost-coded friendship, one I'd often envied. To me John was a brother first, then a friend—exactly the opposite of their relationship.

When they returned, I invited John for dinner the following night and he accepted. Walt gave John a big hug and kissed him on top of his head—their usual way of meeting and parting.

Then Walt said, "Good to have you back home again, man."

We climbed into the van. As we backed out of the driveway, John lifted the shamrock covered paper hat to his chest with one hand and waved to us with his other. He was smiling. The boys and I waved back.

As I write this, sadness overwhelms me. I'm forced to stop writing for a moment, take a deep breath, and blink away tears. "Good-bye John," I say in my head.

It's all still so clear, so vivid in my head. And on the few occasions when I've driven back to his house, I've seen him, still standing there, waving and smiling. Good-bye, good-bye, good-bye.

He seems happy, I thought to myself as we drove to my mother-in-law's. *Happier than he usually is when he comes home from his trips.*

My mother-in-law invited us to return the following evening to celebrate my sister-in-law's birthday. Feeling torn, I initially declined, saying we had already invited John to our house.

"He's not leaving soon again, is he? I mean, he's not going anywhere, is he?" my mother-in-law asked.

"No, I guess not. At least, not that I know of."

After Walter agreed to call John to reschedule the dinner, I finally gave in.

What were John's thoughts and feelings those next six hours, his last? Again, I don't know about his, but I know about mine. I felt restless. As we visited with Walt's family, I was enveloped in a cloud of nagging, unsettled feelings. Something was wrong. I can't explain it, couldn't then, and can't now. Did I sense his death? Or was I feeling guilty at having passed my brother over?

We came home at 8:30. Walt finally called John at 9:30 and asked to change our appointment.

"What did he say?" I yelled up to the loft, where Walt was phoning.

"He said it was okay for Tuesday."

Was it okay? Was he upset? Did he feel rejected, cast aside? A non-priority? I do not know. I do not know. I only know that he left his house a few minutes after that call, then headed to Sumas, Washington. He took a different route than normal to pick up a pair of shoes he'd forgotten earlier at a friend's. Had he not gone to get the shoes, he might not have encountered his "killer" car. Was he lonely? The thought haunted me for a long time after his death.

When I went to bed that night I couldn't sleep for a long time. I began to weep. I wept for John; I still felt so unsettled. I wept at the thought that he was alone in his little house, and *we* had changed our date.

It didn't feel right. It wasn't right. I wondered what John's future was. Would he ever find true fulfillment? I wept until I thought my tears were all used up, then, at long last, fell asleep.

At 2:30 a.m. a knock came on our bedroom window. John was dead. At 10:04 p.m., just thirty minutes after Walt had spoken to him, he had been killed.

While I had wept at the thought of John's aloneness, he was passing from this life to another. Was it a lonely passing, and did he fight it? Were my feelings his? Was he saying good-bye to me? I do not know.

But I do know this (I discovered this a few months after his death): after we had dropped off his car he had called his friend, Neil, in Toronto. It was an unusually long telephone call; his friend was also struck by how lonely John seemed.

This reinforced my own thoughts and feelings, but such thoughts always leave me with suffocating despair. So I've chosen to remember John like this: standing in front of his house, waving, smiling; breathing in the warm, fresh farm air; admiring the blooming daffodils and greening grass.

11:20 p.m. Forty minutes until Good Friday. I'm so tired, but I feel a rush of words in my head. I must commit them to paper before they're buried in all the other debris.

How long is a night? Only those who have spent an entire night awake after receiving the horrifying news of a loved one's sudden death can fully understand what I'm about to say.

2:30 a.m. March 16, 1987. I fall into a restless sleep. My reservoir of tears is empty. My body seems to sense, even to anticipate, what my mind doesn't want to admit. The tears I shed before sleeping are only a trial run.

Nervous hands reach up in the dark, still night and tap on our bedroom window.

"Walt, are you awake? Can you let us in? We have to tell you something." It is Ernie and Margaret, my siblings.

I don't want to hear. *Go away. Go away, bad dream.*

Walt bolts up and sits on the edge of the bed, shaking his head. Like me, he's in a daze. "Who is it?" he calls into the darkness.

"It's me—Ernie. Marg's with me. Can you open the door?"

"Oh, God, God, God. What time is it?" I ask.

"2:30."

My heart thunders in my mouth. *Oh, God, what is it?* I roll out of bed, throw on my housecoat, forgetting to tie the sash, then slide down the hallway. I'm like Jello sitting on a block of ice. *I know, I know something bad has happened.*

"What's wrong? What's happened? *What is wrong?*" I hear a strange voice asking over and over, then realize it is my own. I expect to hear that Mom is sick, Dad's had a heart attack, or worse, that both are dead. These things happen to people my parents' age. But this? Not this!

"John's been in an accident," Marg says, trying to cushion the violent news with her soft voice.

"WHAT?" I yell. "He's not dead, is he?" I shout accusingly, as though they, bearers of this news, are to blame. *"Is he?"* My scream echoes to every corner of the earth.

"Yes, he is." I watch her mouth form the words, see the words reach me, feel them enter me.

"Oh, no, oh, no, this can't be true. Noooo!" I scream and turn to the TV stand. I cling to the corner post, my exposed chest and belly pressed into the wood.

Her words stab me. Blood and tears pour everywhere, soaking into the oil-stained wood. Water and oil don't mix. But here they do, here in this horrible room where time has stood still.

For a long moment I stay there, arms wrapped around that oak beam, as though it will shield me. It doesn't. But someone's arms come from behind and holds me as I cry, our flesh glued together by this unspeakable grief.

And then the realization, the processing of information, and the regurgitation. "It's all my fault, it's all my fault. He wanted to come here today, and we had to go out. He wanted to come here for supper tomorrow, and we changed that, too. When did this happen?"

"At 10:00 o'clock."

"Oh, no, oh, no—Walt just talked to him, just before that. It's our fault."

"Elsie, it is *not* your fault."

"Yes, it is," I sobbed.

"No! He decided to go out tonight and then got hit. It's not your fault. Here, come sit down." My sister led me like a little child to the couch. I stopped midway.

"I have to see him. I want to see him. Where is he? Let's go now. I won't believe till I see him!"

And the final horror. "You can't, Elsie. His car exploded. He's all burnt up."

"Oh, God, no," I wail and sink onto the couch, my face falling into my hands, my body folded in half. I rock and rock, my body shaking in this storm.

"Are you all right, Elsie? Should I get you something? Are you going to faint?" a voice asks.

"No. I'm just so cold, so cold." The elements have entered my house, uninvited. *Get thee behind me . . .*

Someone wraps my quilt around me. It makes no difference. A north wind howls inside my body. What could ever thaw such cold?

"She's in shock," my sister says, from far away.

Old events now work their way to the front of my mind and collide with this latest news; like debris they fly into the air around me.

Erv said that car was a deathtrap. . . . He brought it out last weekend. . . . John had parked it at the airport in Chilliwack. Oh no! I filled the tank with gas on Friday. Now the whole thing exploded. Oh, now it's all my fault. Oh, God, this can't be true. Oh, no—the family picture, the one we took last August—why, oh, why, didn't he come home for that? Now we have to look at him glued in the corner by himself for the rest of our lives.

The image of the family portrait lures me back to reality. I suddenly realize that this grief is not only my own. There are others grieving too. My parents—how would they ever cope?

"Oh, God—Mom and Dad. How are they doing?"

"Not well."

"Who's with them now?

"Charlotte's there."

"I have to go to them. I have to tell them that we saw John this afternoon, that he was happy, that Walt talked to him tonight, just before he died. Can you tell them for me?" For a moment it is as if John were resurrected—but only for a moment.

Walt sits beside me, a stone. No cry or sound has come from him since the news. He just sits and stares. A petrified piece of humanity. Where did he go in those few minutes, that whole night?

"I knew," he told me later, "I knew the minute they knocked on the window that John was dead."

We were the last to know, Walt and I, of all the siblings in Clearbrook. I suppose in a sense we were the most difficult to tell—we were the closest to John.

They came together, Marg and Ernie. They didn't phone to tell us the news like they had each other. They faced us with the news, then opened wide their arms, putting aside for a few minutes their own shattered grief, to help us carry our own. For that I shall ever be grateful to them.

"I love you guys," I say. We embrace.

How long can one night be? Long. Beyond imagination.

Marg and Ernie left. It was only 3:15 a.m. Afterward, Walt and I sat riveted, each frozen in our own thoughts. Crazy thoughts. I looked down and realized my housecoat was wide open. *If only*, I thought, *if only I had remembered to close my housecoat, maybe then it wouldn't have hurt so much. Maybe then the wound would not have gone so deep. Maybe then I could have kept my blood inside.*

"Should I make some tea?" I ask, partly because I feel it might help thaw my body, partly because I don't know what else to do. What should one do? Sleep was out of the question. So was talking—where would I find words to speak? So I made some tea. I drank mine while Walt only stared at his.

What happens on the inside is often different from what happens on the outside. Outside, the person sips tea and wanders around the house.

Inside, storms brew. *This is a lie. It can't be true that you are dead! This is a lie. Take me to the bathroom, I need to puke, to puke, to puke. Let me go outside and scream. I'll wake the world and tell them all that "John is dead!" I'll scream until I'm hoarse, until all the pain is gone, until the tears and blood have stopped. This is a lie that you are dead.*

Inside, I thought I'd go mad that night. Outside, I worked hard to keep my inside in, to make my body a dike against a raging tide. Is that how people go crazy, by turning inside out?

I didn't let go, though that might have been easier than facing the storm. Instead, I walked around the house, always ending in front of the family portrait, where John's face sat alone in the bottom, left-hand corner. Away from the rest of us—forever now.

"Why? Why? Why did he have to go out tonight?" I ask Walt over and over, speaking into his chest.

"I don't know, Els, I don't know," he replied, his words rolling over my head.

Oh yes, that night was long. Every second an hour, every minute a day, every hour a year. It was a lifetime long. I had entered a long, dark tunnel of timelessness. When I thought that surely it must nearly be over, it was only five minutes. And then I'd wait a long, long time to look again. But again, only five minutes had passed.

I waited for dawn. Somehow, it seemed that with the coming of daylight everything would be all right. John might not be dead after all.

I wandered all night. Strange how your feelings alter in grief. You feel almost no fatigue. In fact, you feel everything as nothing. Death petrifies, no, *murders* feelings.

At 5:30 a.m. Walt fell asleep on the couch. I went upstairs to our loft, where so very recently the three of has had sat together, sharing music and laughter by candlelight.

"Aren't you coming up?" John had asked. I had just curled up with a book. But this time, for some reason, I had abandoned it and joined the two of them upstairs.

Now, as I sat writing a list of friends to call, I saw him sitting in the rocking chair, head leaned back, a glass in one hand, a cigarette in the other. Are you here, John? Where are you, John? ARE YOU SLEEPING? ARE YOU SLEEPING, BROTHER JOHN?

2

The Sting
of Death

February 23, 1988

What shall I recount tonight, as I listen to Mozart's Requiem? Which part shall be the least painful? And how can I say any of it adequately? There is no language to describe the hell that enters your soul, that permeates your entire mind and body when death occupies your home.

If I could have entered my screams, never to return, I would have. Is that how people go crazy? I wonder— how do you let yourself enter that other world? Is it a conscious decision?

I remember the look I saw recently on a mother's face as she stepped from the hearse and walked to the grave of her five-year-old son. Like John, he was killed by a drunk driver. The woman looked then like I now felt, like a living groan.

Before calling John's friends, I wandered around our house. "Mommy, what's wrong? Why is there so much crying?" Daniel, my oldest son, called from his bedroom.

I went into Daniel's bedroom and lay beside him,

holding him tight. *I will keep you safe, my son.*

"What's wrong, Mommy? Why are you crying so loud?" he asked again.

"Oh, Daniel," I said, wondering what words to use. "Uncle John has been killed. He's dead. That means you won't ever see him again. He'll never come over again."

"Never, Mommy?"

"Never, Daniel."

Daniel's response surprised me. "Well, I guess he's with Jonah [John's dog] now. First, Jonah got killed in a car crash. Now, Uncle John."

What did I expect, that he should break down and cry like me? How could he understand at five that *never* was permanent? The uncle he loved so much and always asked for had been ripped, without permission, from his life.

After a while, I tucked him in and left the room. My two beautiful *alive* sons. What if this should be their fate as well?

At 5:30 a.m. I made a list of whom to call. I even tried dialing a few numbers. No answer, except for one, a childhood friend of John's. He didn't believe my words. We talked briefly

God, this is too hard. I can't do this. I don't want to have to convince people that John is dead. You have to take this from me. I'm going to go crazy. I stared at the list and the phone for a long time, then went downstairs, got dressed, and went to the van.

I drove to the local donut shop to tell Walt's employer Walt wouldn't be at work that day.

"Elsie," he said, as he saw me coming.

"John's dead. He was in a car crash last night. Do you need anything from our house? I mean, Walt won't be coming to work today." I struggled to say the words. *This is a recording. This is a recording. John is dead.*

"Oh gee," I heard from his direction. "Was that down by the border?"

"Yeah."

"Well, tell Walt not to worry."

I turned away, thinking how indifferent he had seemed. But as I started my van and looked up, I saw him sitting there, cup on the table, his hands rubbing his eyes. Shock, I realized, had prompted his response. This was one behavior etiquette books had forgotten to address.

I drove away, barely able to see the road, to shift gears, to steer. I traveled in the eye of the storm to the scene of the accident, the origin of my glacial state. Perhaps I thought I'd meet him or find his ghost along the way. I'm still not certain why I made that trek.

Down South Fraser Way, to McCallum, to Vye. Down the steep hill, and south down C Street, to the border. No car anywhere, no evidence at all.

"They could at least have left the car there so we could see it, " I heard an angry voice—my own—say. I didn't know then that I hadn't driven the same route, didn't know his car had rested a couple hundred feet north, not south, of Vye.

I changed direction; my next destination his house, Why, I didn't know. I just followed my inner compass again.

Once there, I stayed in the van for a few minutes. This would be the final moment of truth. I walked into his porch, where his kitchen sink was. It was filled with dirty dishes. Someone lived here! A key lay on the counter. I picked it up, unlocked the door, and let myself in. It was as though he had left it there for me.

"John, are you here?" I called. *Oh John, is this really true? How can this be? I talked to you just yesterday.*

I slowly wandered through the house, looking, looking. He was not there. Nobody here, just evidence of recent inhabitance.

In the kitchen, a potful of alphabet soup stood on the stove, a dirty bowl beside it. An opened newspaper lay on the living room floor. On a table beside the stereo stood a family portrait, a picture of John with my two boys, and a transformer airplane. A guitar case lay on the floor.

In his bedroom lay his suitcase, open, but not yet unpacked. His dresser was covered with birthday cards from friends. "Have a good year, John" and "We love you!" they screamed into the vacant room. In the corner lay a garbage bag, full of dirty laundry. An unused Mexican blanket lay draped over the chair.

Back in the kitchen, the table held an opened letter, dirty cutlery, and piles of unopened correspondence. Unattended business.

I sat down at the kitchen table and looked around. *John, John, where are you?* The silence of the house answered, *I am not here.*

I sat a while longer, memorizing the rooms around me, inhaling the smells and memories of this place John had vacated.

I shall take this with me when I leave this house. All the things I cannot touch and hold can still stay inside of me. They shall never leave me.

The next days blurred by, details of weather, food, and world events not grasped. I remember only the sound I woke up to each morning. It was made by my mouth, or rather, exited via my mouth. It came from deep inside, from a cave, from the vacuum John's death had caused.

It was the sound of sin, an evil sound. Not a human sound, but the savage sound of a badly wounded animal shrieking, lashing out against the pain of entrapment. This cry was no civilized response. It frightened even me.

That is how I awoke, to the sound of my own barbaric cries. No quilt or pillow could contain the noise I made. No medication could tame the animal in me, raging against the sin that killed my John. But my cries were not only my own. They were joined by the sounds God made when death first took a life.

Three days I woke like this. Each time Walt rushed to our bed and held me close, my back to his front. My unborn child lay thrashing in front; I couldn't even face the man who tried to comfort me. But it helped. It helped to fit myself inside his arms. He was my only hope to fight the urge to let the beast within devour me. Daniel and Matthew were with others, away from all this sin and pain.

My husband and my unborn child—they held the light so I could find my way back out. The child inside me pitched and thundered. "See," she whispered, "there is life. Come back, come back. For me." I did; how could I not?

My eyes and ears tuned in again to the sounds and smells of life. The phone, ringing, ringing, with messages of "we're thinking of you." Knocking, knocking, on the door, which was opened to receive a garden of flowers from friends. No sin here, only the smell of comfort, the sight of rainbows, and a divine promise: "*I will not leave you.*"

I clung to them all, to the sounds, the smells, the sights. But I remember no details and few words. Only arms and shoulders, comings and goings, rivers of tears. And the miracle: the comforted becoming comforters. "He loved you so much," I told his friends.

Death has so many faces. Here it wed the mourners. It made us one, this group of hundreds, crying out against an evil force.

If only that were all, to sit and cry and comfort. But

death brings more, especially in our culture. Choosing the coffin. Planning the funeral. Ordering food for after the service. These are the requirements for a marriage such as this.

I did little. The animal inside had bound me too tightly. I couldn't play my part in this unscheduled drama. No dress rehearsals here to smooth the wrinkles, to sharpen the lines.

What could I give as my last gift? I chose to write the eulogy. The final words, the final act of John's life story, the hardest, yet simplest, words I ever wrote. While others chose hymns and Scripture verses, I summarized John's life.

I rose before the dawn the day before we buried him, the third day after his death. I made him come alive inside each word. This, I thought, this was my brother John. This *is* my brother John. I *was* my brother's keeper.

"Happy flying, John" I closed his story; I left no period. John was *not* dead; he rose inside my words. The body we would lay to rest, but John? *NO!* He did not die. He is not there. John is risen.

3

The Horror
of Death

Death is so difficult, especially for the survivors. For the one who has died, everything is over. It is finished. At least that's what we have been taught to believe—that death is the end of physical pain, anxiety, and fear. For the survivors, such thoughts are a great comfort, especially when the victim has endured a long battle against pain.

For those of us whose loved ones have died a sudden, violent, or gruesome death, there is always the temptation to visualize the final moments. We are drawn to the moments between impact and death, when we imagine a consciousness remained, an awareness of pain.

I have tried to externalize my visualizations by poetic expression. Doing so eases my internal pain, even making me feel, sometimes, as if a physical weight is lifting from my heart and mind.

My brother died a horrible death. A speeding Dodge hit his VW beetle head-on. John's car spun around several times. Then, bouncing to the shoulder of the road, it exploded.

The accident occurred at 10:04 p.m. John's body was removed at 12:00 p.m. The flames were extinguished as quickly as possible. But the hot metal prevented the firefighters from touching it, even with the jaws of life.

And so his charred, broken body rested on the metal remains of the steering wheel. It returned, as rigor mortis set in, to its prebirth, fetal position.

I try to imagine the difficulty of removing such a body from that car. I imagine the horror of transporting such a body to the hospital morgue, and pronouncing "it" dead. I imagine the horror of that twenty-eight-year-old doctor, seeing that black mass of humanity, asking for a name. I imagine the feelings of the coroner and pathologist as they pry teeth loose to "positively identify" this "person."

And finally, I imagine the horror of the pathologist as he comes face to face with John, and the imagining fills me, too, with horror.

Then the final scenario. The hearse arrives with body inside at its second-last destination—the funeral home. This cargo horrifies and perplexes the undertakers. What can they do with this? And how should they do it?

The family arrives, clothes in hand. "Please," says the brother who has accompanied both parents. "Please, we'd like him fully clothed." They hand him a white shirt, black suede jacket, dark underwear, gray pants and belt, gray socks, black shoes, and a red tie.

He takes their burden gently, then says, "We'll do our best."

"Then," says the father, "we'd like to see him."

"Oh, but sir, I wouldn't advise it; it's pretty awful."

"It doesn't matter. I have to, want to, see him. Then I'll know for certain it is him, that he is really dead."

The family leaves. The undertaker is riveted to that spot for a long, long time. He watches the family go out the front door, get into their car, and slowly drive away, red tail lights disappearing into misty haze. He calls a meeting with the other employees. "What shall we do?" he says. "They want to see him."

Back home, I hid downstairs and began writing John's eulogy. Embracing all the good things, I gave John the final tribute he deserved.

That evening we all drove to the funeral home. Walt and I arrived first. We sat in the van, listening to J. J. Cale, John's tape. I clung to a box of Kleenex, while my tears competed with the rain outside. Inside my womb my child thrashed, its restless maneuverings matching my own.

Silently, as though in slow motion, we left the safety of our vehicles and proceeded down that long walkway.

"Is this the Klassen family?" the man in the dark pin-striped suit asked, as we came into the foyer.

"Yes."

"Please come this way."

God, I want to wake up now. This is a cruel dream. Please.

But no one shook my shoulders. They only took my hands and led me to a chair. "Are you okay, Elsie? How's the baby?"

"Still kicking," I replied. My hands clenched into fists at my side and opened only long enough to brush the tears from my cheeks. My icy fingers touched the hot water on my face and recoiled, clenched tight again, then withdrew into the safety of my warm coat pockets.

My oldest brother left the room. He came back with the undertaker, who stood silent beside my brother, his hands entwined in front of his stomach.

"Okay," said my brother, as he stood before us. "Here's what's going to happen." He spoke in short, almost staccato spurts.

My mind focused again and I heard him talking; heard

the instructions for viewing the "viewable," the foot. The rest, though broken, had been clothed, so the family could still see his outline.

I couldn't go. I wanted to, desperately, but an inner voice kept saying, "The baby. You have to think of the baby." So I stayed, sitting in a chair in that pretend "living room" with its love seats, couch, padded wing chairs, and strategically placed oak end tables with flowered Kleenex boxes.

My brother and his wife sat next to me, holding hands. "He liked you guys so much," I heard myself saying.

"I know, I know," Bev said, and gently drew my fist into her warm hand, where I let it sit and felt it slowly wind itself between her fingers. My brother sat silent, chewing his lower lip, his motions stopping only when he cleared his throat or coughed.

A silent moment passed between us. It was broken by the sound from the other room, a collective wail and weeping. *So now it's done. They've seen him. I wonder how he looks.*

"I don't want to see him," my brother said. "I just want to remember him the way he was."

"That's the best way, for all of us," his wife replied.

"I'd like to," I whispered, "but the baby."

Footsteps, then a voice.

"Did you wish to join your family now?"

We stood simultaneously, not replying, silently following.

So this is it. This is it, I thought, as I marched down the aisle to the coffin, bedecked with blood-red roses, snowy carnations, and baby's breath.

My family stood in clusters, red-eyed, clutching soppy Kleenexes.

"Komm," my mother said. She guided me to where it

stood. I reached out and patted the place where I knew John's head to be.

"I love you, John" I said. I visualized his smiling face. Warm brown eyes. Moustache—the bridge between nose and upper lip. Bristly suntanned cheeks and chin. Unkempt, windblown, thinning head of hair.

I saw that dark brown, curly hair. I remembered his hands and fingers running through it—front to back, front to back, causing, not a smoother head of hair, but an even more disheveled look. His hair stood straight up, revealing the full extent of his receding hairline. I felt John then as I envisioned him, as I knew and remembered him. Again I spoke, this time oblivious to those around me.

"I love you, John. So very, very much. I hope you know that. Always remember that. You were so special. I hope when I die people will say about me what they've been saying about you."

"They will, they will," my mother said behind me.

"I wish you didn't have to die. I would have died for you, you know. I would have taken your place so you could finish off the things you wanted to."

"He wouldn't have wanted that, Elsie, you know that. Your children need you," my mother said.

"You were a great guy, John. I'm going to miss you so much. I love you. Bye, John."

I stood for a long time, stroking the dark, smooth wood of his expensive coffin above his precious head. Then I finally turned away. Gravity had ceased for me. I floated through the room weightless, directionless.

My father took me in his arms and whispered things to me I don't remember. I laid my head against his shoulder and wept, while he gently stroked my hair. I was a child again, protected, taken care of. I wished to be forever enfolded by my parents, where pain could never catch me again.

Another pair of hands reached out and wrapped me in familiar arms. My husband. The veil had lifted. I was once again adult, wife, mother. *Pain.*

The moment passed, the tears receded. In grief you do what must be done. The coffin was moved to the adjoining room where we filed around it, taking photos. Mom and Dad, click; siblings, click; siblings with parents, click; siblings, spouses, and parents, click; each couple alone, click—except Walt and I, we refused.

Then at last the coffin alone. Click, click, click. "Did you get the cross behind it?" my father asked.

It is finished. We retreat to the pews, staring at the coffin, the flowers, and the photo of John. He stands in it beside his plane, HGBG, grinning, leaning against the dove emblazoned on its tail. In the bottom corner of the photo, my father places a sticker. It is a duplicate of the one John put on his plane's tail: "Smile, God loves you."

The room is mostly silent, the only sounds an occasional sniffle, cough, or whisper. Then suddenly, there is a wailing. "It's so unfair, it's such a waste." My oldest brother's grief surfaces.

His wife leans over, holds him tight and rocks him, crying too. "I know, I know," she says.

I look at them in disbelief, imprisoned by my own grief. I cannot go to him as others do, surrounding him, comforting him. I wince as I look again at the coffin. *This cannot, cannot be.*

Our family is calm once more. But only briefly. Now my mother rises and stands before the coffin. She begins to pray in German, in a quivering but remarkably strong voice. "Oh, God, you have given us the gift of John. We thank you for his earthly life, and now we offer him back to you. We ask for strength. Amen."

She weeps openly for a minute, then takes a deep breath, wipes her eyes, and says in her broken English,

"So John would say, 'Mom, stop crying.' Let's go." With that, she motions us to follow. We stand and, one at a time, follow her out of that place into the cold, dark, rainy night to our cars. That part is over.

This is as far as I can write today. The rest must still be recorded. But not today. My mind says stop.

4

Burial
or Resurrection?

Family gatherings will never be the same. On March 19, 1987, we gathered for the last time in the basement of our parents' church, where long ago we had all attended Sunday school.

There were fourteen of us that day, spouses and offspring included. As we did long ago, we came dressed in our Sunday best. Even John, who rarely dressed up, had been dressed in his best. Only this time he was lying down, upstairs. No snide remarks today, no sarcasm. Only deathly silence.

Someone has made a circle of chairs for us to sit on while we wait for our cue to go onstage. I am not there, though my body is—all dressed in pink, the same dress I wore the last time John and I were together. Let the others wear black. I wear the color of life. I will not cry, at least not in front of the others.

I am not here. I'm flying high above, watching others cry. I cannot even feel my face. "Are you alright, Elsie?" someone asks. "Your face is white."

"I'm not sure," I answer truthfully. *I am not here. I will not cry. I will live through this.*

"We can go upstairs now," the pastor tells us.

A hand takes mine. Obediently I follow. Up the stairs. We stand a moment, then the long walk. *Look at all these people, John. Can you believe this? The church is full. Your show's sold out!*

Someone rolls the coffin to the sanctuary entrance. The family stands behind it two by two, arms linked, one carrying the other as the procession begins. Christopher Parkening plays prerecorded numbers on his classical guitar for us as we begin our descent.

"Whoosh!" The crowd stands in unison. Like a flock of migrating birds they lift off their pews, five hundred souls rising to show their respect for us, the grieving family. We float atop the cushion of their flight, carried by their love and mutual mourning.

We land on two front pews. We are soldiers facing battle. Who will win? Life or death? The army facing us is only flowers. Thousands line the front, surrounding the casket which holds captive our brother, son, and friend. Who can fight a war on grounds like these?

The only blood shed here comes in the form of tears. *I will not cry. I will not fight. I am not here. I'm lying in that box beside my brother. No! I will not die. I am instead among the flowers, surrounded by the smell of life. I am not here; I'm high above.*

The words I wrote at dawn the day before have fueled my flight. John is not gone, his fight was won two thousand years before he walked this earth. I do not need to cry. I *would* believe.

The pastor speaks.

> Do you not know?
> Have you not heard?
> The Lord is the everlasting God,

the Creator of the ends of the earth.
He will not grow tired or weary,
  and his understanding no one can fathom.
He gives strength to the weary
  and increases the power of the weak.
Even youths grow tired and weary,
  and young men stumble and fall;
but those who hope in the Lord
  will renew their strength.
They will soar on wings like eagles;
  they will run and not grow weary,
  they will walk and not be faint
                              (Isaiah 40:28-31, NIV).

I sing the songs, I sing them all, each note, each phrase, because I know "It *is* well with my soul."

Funerals are really like dreams. You visit them, then wake and find yourself inside a big white car. "Where are we going?" asks the man in front, wearing a chauffeur hat.

My father hands out mints. Scotch mints. The kind he used to give us on the way to church. This time one is left inside his pocket. Who will suck and crunch that extra candy now?

The cemetery lies ahead. A pile of dirt guards the hole dug the day before. *This is where it ends?*

We file around the hole. "Ashes to ashes, dust to dust," the pastor reads, then says a prayer.

The sound of planes drown out his prayer. All eyes open, looking up instead of down. "It's called the 'Missing Man Formation'," my brother yells above the noise. The gap in the triad where there once were four is now filled with wailing. We stand and watch and weep.

And then another flight comes overhead. "It's the 'Victory Formation'," yells someone. John's plane is inhabited by someone else, a friend. There is hope! We focus on the ground again.

More hugs and tears are shared around the hole until at last the crowd grows thin. Our family crowds around once more. We take apart the flowers on John's coffin. One solitary rose is all we leave. John stays behind, surrounded by celestial flowers and unseen gardens.

But knowing and believing this does not erase human thoughts and feelings. "Now we have to leave him there, alone," my father says through tears, as we return to church for the reception.

"Shhh," my mother says. He falls silent. No mints are passed this time, not even the one left over. It occupies a space in my father's pocket which it shall never leave.

The dream I thought I woke from when we drove inside that car isn't over. It is a dream inside a dream. We arrive at church again and once again are buoyed upon loving arms. "Sit here," they say. We do.

The meal is fine, we force it down, then sit back, waiting for the crowd to resurrect our John through anecdotes and memories. It works. We laugh and cry and reminisce until we find the strength to draw the curtain.

The crowd thins. Alone again: the family.
"Take these and these," my parents say, dispensing food and flowers not taken by others.

That night we meet once more. Again chairs form a circle in our parents' house. Again we laugh and resurrect John; our war against the coming empty days kept one more night at bay.

I think, *Oh, good, the worst is over. Now I'll feel myself again.* But I am wrong.

I wake once more in death's dark shadow. We face the truth, the life John left behind in his small house.

I drive the route I'd driven all my life, two empty boxes by my side—they were all I had. *How foolish can you be?* I ask myself when I arrive and see my sister with several dozen.

"Where shall we start?" we say in unison.

"I'll start here," she says.

"And I'll go there."

How do you pack a life away in boxes? With pain, with pain. Each item wrapped in boxes cushioned only with tears.

Each jar and can is held and smelled and opened; each plate and cup examined. Each blanket, sheet, and pillow is touched, caressed, each shirt is held against one's face. Photos, cradled in one's hands, are gently laid aside. And always, always, everything is done in awe, for packing away another's life is treading on holy ground.

We come without an invitation. We do our task without permission. We enter John's most private world, a place where only a few had ever visited.

It doesn't take as long as expected. John's house is small. John's identity hadn't rested primarily on his possessions, though they offered clues. The boxes of tapes, records, music books, and novels easily outnumber those containing linens and dishes.

And one box alone isn't enough to contain the many letters, cards, and pictures. They fall out of books and pockets, suitcases and guitar case, drawers and closets. They are everywhere. Obviously not all of John's friends were at his funeral. His correspondence is postmarked from all over the world.

Here, through his possessions, John gives us his final message, as we clean and pack and file. It is an honor to share in that last purging of his physical life.

Another task of death is over. John's house now is skeletal; the soul has left. The house is cleaner than he ever kept it. There's a vacancy where he once lived.

Now to face life without him. No script or lines to follow his last act. I'm glad I didn't know how hard this play would be.

My
Photo Album

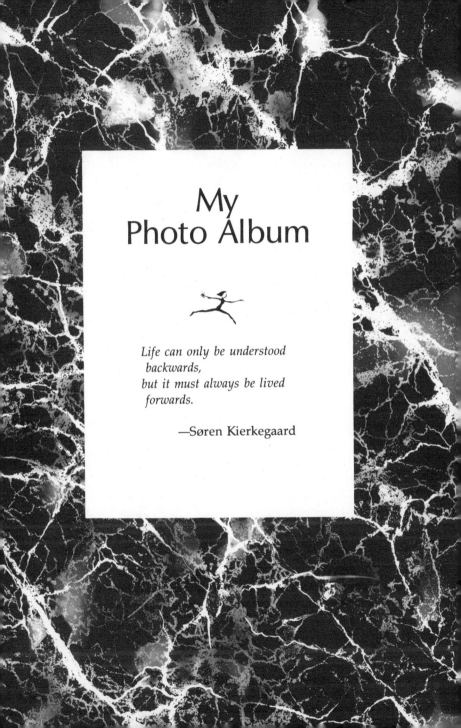

*Life can only be understood
backwards,
but it must always be lived
forwards.*

—Søren Kierkegaard

5

Growing-up Years

February 29, 1988

Nearly a year has passed. "You are in our prayers during this difficult time," I read as I thumb through my scrapbook of sympathy cards.

"In this difficult time." What does that mean? How long am I allowed to have a difficult time? A week? A month? A year? Twenty years? As long as I'm alive my brother will be dead. That is difficult and always will be.

"Time will heal the sorrow but the loss will remain for us here on earth," I read in a card from a woman who buried her little boy a year before John died. *She knows*, I thought. *She knows my thoughts, and feelings.* With guilt I suddenly remember—did I not promise her my prayers?

I look again at the woman's card. On the front, surrounded by a myriad of blue butterflies, it says, "The Lord will give strength unto his people and bless his people with peace." Yes, I have experienced the presence, strength, and peace of God. Still I am made of flesh, and long to be touched at times by the flesh of other people. Sometimes I wish at least they'd ask.

Perhaps they are afraid to ask, or don't know what to ask. So now I'll tell them all. I'll tell them how it was, how it is, and how it will be.

Kierkegaard said that "life can only be understood backwards; but it must always be lived forwards." This is the purpose of my remembering, to understand the past in the context of the present, then to move on.

When I open my photo album now, I don't merely open a book with pages filled with photos. I enter a door to a hallway, a long hallway with many more doors, each leading into a roomful of memories.

Memories of a childhood when we played happily and endlessly together. Memories of a painful time when sibling rivalry and differences threatened to overwhelm love. And finally, the happier memories of recent times, when, not only blood ties, but true friendship joined us. In adulthood my bond with John deepened; my husband and children each provided links in the strong chain which bound us all together.

Walk with me into this hallway. Hold my hand, and I'll lead you through the doors. Don't be afraid of what I'll say or do. And don't—please don't—be afraid of your own tears and fears. If you wish to laugh or cry, or even both, do. It doesn't bother me; I've learned to do both too. That's how I cope.

When I come to doors that have been locked forever by John's sudden death, weep with me, comfort me. Then go to your own life's halls and open your doors.

Though I've learned to appreciate the rooms full of memories that John's life left me, I'd still give anything to have him back, to ask him for the key to all those bolted doors.

That I can never do. And so I show you the memories.

First, a black-and-white photo of a family of six in front of a small, white house. At the bottom of the picture is a date: July '57. My brother John is in front on a tricycle. He is two and a half and looks ready for take-off. His hands are on the handle bars. His feet rest on the pedals. He looks very serious. Behind stand his sister, two brothers, and his father and mother. His mother is nearly nine months pregnant with my twin brother and me.

Here in this picture we have not yet connected physically; our only common dwelling thus far is the womb. Here is the first house he lived in, which, ironically, was also his address when he died. Here is John's *alpha* and *omega*, his beginning and his end. And here, in this picture, John and I are on the brink of meeting.

In this album I find no clues to what John did when he first saw my twin and me. Did he laugh or cry—or hit us? Did he ignore us? Was he more concerned with his toys and play than with two new bundles of mewling humanity? I don't know nor does it matter much, for as I flip the pages, I see much evidence of our times together.

It is winter. Snow covers the hill across the road from the farm on which we lived. "Dominoe's Hill" we called it, because it belonged to Mr. Dominoe, who lived at the corner of our dead-end road. He owned the whole east side of our street. We often heard the story of how he used to own even more land, before the Trans-Canada Highway severed it, making our street a dead-end road. For as long as I can remember a "no exit" sign has stood at the corner of our Gladwin Road, where it intersected with King Road and the rest of the world.

So there we are, at the top of the hill, four of us, waving at the cameraman. We're all smiling. There are two toboggans. John and my twin, Ernie, are on one. I and our neighbor, also named John, are on the other. We're all bundled up in thick cloth coats—we didn't have ski jackets then. The three boys are wearing toques (*pushelmitzen* we called them in German) and I'm wearing a kerchief.

The sight of that kerchief brings back ugly memories of my grade-school years, when all the other girls in my school wore store-bought clothes. The kerchief was my ultimate badge of distinction. Even John noticed how out of place my clothing was in that school. Once, when I was ten and in fifth grade, I shared a classroom with John, who was twelve and in seventh grade. John was going through an intense preadolescence, and it irritated him immensely that we were together all day.

Already then, I was a witness and reporter, carrying his misdeeds home with me and spilling them on the kitchen table for my parents to see. He hated that.

But back to the kerchief and the clothing. I recall one particular day, walking home from school with John. I was wearing a home-sewn dress, made of nondescript blue rayon, with floppy white lace around the collar, wrists, and waist. It was my almost-favorite. I thought it looked quite nice.

Then John glared at me and said, "Why do you always wear that ugly dress?"

I was shattered, not only by his criticism, but also by the realization that he was ashamed of me.

Later on, of course, during high school years, I redeemed myself. Often when John brought his friends home from school, I'd hear them say with undisguised admiration, "Is that your sister?" And the ultimate irony is that I eventually married one of his best friends.

The photo of the four of us in toboggans leads also to nicer memories of the countless hours we played together in those first years of our lives.

Beyond Dominoe's Hill was a forest where we played "War" and "Lost," rested on damp moss-covered logs, dug into anthills. Finally, we came out again, rolling down the hill, then racing to the fence which separated Mr. Dominoe's land from the rest of our neighborhood, dodging the cow pies which dotted that vast playground.

Did Mr. Dominoe mind? I don't know, but I do remember the feeling of terror in my stomach when I saw him coming, always carrying a stick. Now I realize it was probably meant for chasing the cows to the barn, not for the four of us, sitting on the branches of his black cherry tree in the heat of those summer evenings.

"Mr. Dominoe's coming!" I would yell to the others, who had clambered high above me. I'd sit closer to the bottom, my face always turned toward the end of the road where Mr. Dominoe's house dominated the horizon.

"Who cares?" my brother John would yell back. He would continue popping the juicy, night-black cherries into his mouth. His voice would sound tough and determined, but always with my call he'd slowly descend. He would jump from the bottom branch just as Mr. Dominoe got within arm's reach.

I, on the other hand, would by this time be safe on our front lawn. I would watch as John dashed for the fence, wiggled under the bottom row of barbed wire, or clambered up and over, running, laughing, face and hands stained a dark purple, his tongue licking the last juice from around his mouth.

Mr. Dominoe would stand by the tree, shaking his stick in our direction, yelling in Russian.

John's antics on that cherry tree were mere foreshadowings. Already in his teen years, and habitually in his adult life, John was last to arrive at a party, last to come home for chores, and predictably late serving meals to his dinner guests. "*Mañana*" he'd always reply with a gigantic grin when anyone confronted him. Ironic that in death he should go first.

John exemplified spontaneity and enthusiasm throughout his life. At his funeral a friend recalled a different cherry tree. John had invited a group of friends over for a barbecue and, typically, had forgotten a few last-minute items. A friend went back with John.

Just as they were leaving the driveway, John looked at him and asked, "Hey, want to go raid a cherry tree?"

The friend, feeling awkward about keeping John's guests waiting, protested. Then caught up in John's enthusiasm he agreed, "Sure, I like cherries."

An hour later the two returned, less hungry and clearly happier than when they'd left.

That was John. He savored each moment. You couldn't rush John. He lived in his own time. He always stopped to pick cherries along the way.

The cherry tree represented other things for John as well. Throughout his life John enjoyed taking risks. He often flew on nearly empty gas tanks. Once, en route to Mexico, he was forced to land at night on a sandy beach in California. "Is your tank full, John?" was a question anyone boarding John's plane learned to ask.

Going to John's house for dinner, guests learned to expect it an hour late. Once, when Walt and I arrived for dinner, John was still out buying groceries for the meal! We had to break into his house through the basement door. After that, we always had a snack before we left home.

But though he was often late, John always came through. His plane always landed safely, even if not always at an airport. And his meals were always excellent.

The cherry tree is gone now, and the old piazza-like barn which stood beside it. In its place stands a shiny new barn filled with sweet hay and racehorses. Today our playground is divided into three farms.

And Dominoe's Hill? Still there, but no longer a place

for tobogganing. It's inhabited now by two houses, almost side by side, sitting precisely where we used to launch our waxed, wooden sleds.

Things change. Again, the uncanny *alpha* and *omega*. The McMichaels, Jim and Betty, live there now. And though they are our parents' age, John found in them a deep and lasting friendship. Here he returned for many years, to visit them, to laugh with them, to dream with them, and sometimes to vent his frustrations with them.

He, the only one of us four, returned to Dominoe's Hill. The innocence of our childhood had long since passed, but he returned and built a whole new house of memories with friends who had built their house atop his old one.

Another picture. Again, the four of us, together as in the previous picture. Only this time we're on tricycles, riding down the middle of our dead-end Gladwin Road. This too was part of our vast playground, for when there is little traffic on your street it soon becomes a highway to adventure.

I remember the day the news came that they were going to pave Gladwin Road. A wave of excitement crashed through our neighborhood as we envisioned our own private, roller-skating rink.

The day we heard the trucks and steamroller approach was indescribably exciting. We walked to the end of the road and stood watching, in awe of these mighty municipal workers who were about to alter our playground forever.

With bated breath we watched them heat their giant barrels of black tar, then spread it like paste on our once potholed road. We could practically feel the wind in our ears, as we dreamed of flying down that long, smooth stretch of blacktop magic.

And then the whistling stopped. We watched, with

gloomy faces, as a fleet of dump trucks descended on the hot black tar and dumped their cargo—millions of thumbnail-sized pebbles. They left our road, our roller-skating rink, a stretch of lumpy, bumpy asphalt. We tried to skate there, but the pace was too slow; we soon relegated our skates to unfinished basements, where they quietly rusted away.

Our farm, though small—a mere 10 acres—seemed mammoth at that time. Behind the barns was a thick forest, five acres of it. The forest, together with the neighbors' uncultivated acreage, provided another playground. I remember well those endless treks after school into "the bush," where we forged new paths between the thick oak and countless birch trees. Then, when we reached the other side, we would climb over the barbed wire fence and run through the meadow until we came to the pond.

"Where did you go?" our mother would ask, and we'd reply, "The pond." We would come home late, at dusk, frozen to the core. Our pants and socks clung to our goose-bumped skin where the muddy water had splashed us. We had rowed our rafts to the little island in the middle of the pond, which seemed like an ocean to us.

In winter we spent endless hours skating on the frozen pond, with or without skates—it didn't matter much. What we really liked best was warming up afterward by the bonfire my two older brothers built. Then all of us would hover near the flames, sipping hot, homemade cocoa from our orange thermoses.

There are a few more pictures of that innocent, care-free childhood on this page of my album.

January 1965. John is ten years old in this picture, where we stand high on the chicken-barn roof. I'm leaning over, clinging with one hand to the boards already nailed down, smiling bravely at the cameraman. Dad and my brothers Henry and Ernie are standing straight and tall. And John? John is bent forward, nail in left hand, hammer in right, appearing very industrious. So unlike him—he preferred nonintensive labor.

And the other irony was that John feared heights! Yet he dreamed of becoming a pilot, a dream he realized as an adult. Once again the circle closes. Where does it begin and where does it end?

Two more pictures, both taken at mealtimes. The first is at an extended family gathering. John looks six or so. There are twelve children squeezed around a kitchen table—the British Columbia cousins. The other twenty lived in eastern Canada.

At the back of the photo, John's shining, smiling face leans forward, straining to see. His right hand holds a forkful of food. How typical! Always he had a lust for food matched only by his lust for life.

Perhaps the second photo reveals this desire more clearly. There, at a picnic table in a park in Penticton, British Columbia (we were on a family vacation), sits John. He is looking up, while practically colliding with a large piece of watermelon.

John loved food. He would eat a heaping plateful, savoring each mouthful, making it last longer than you'd think possible. All the while he would carry on a lively, humorous conversation, spiked with an occasional "This is really good!" or "What's in this?"

Then, when I would think he had enough, he would lift his empty plate and ask, "Is there more?" He would fill his plate again, set it down, lean back a moment, and begin eating again. All eyes would watch!

Near the end his pace would decrease. He would pause momentarily, pat his stomach, open his belt another notch, laugh with the people watching him, take a deep breath, then finally lean forward, and eat until his plate was bare.

"So what's for dessert?" he'd ask. We would all burst into laughter.

That vacation was one of only a handful we could afford. We were, after all, a large (seven children) and not well-to-do farm family. We learned to savor moments of holidays, rather than consecutive days away from the farm. An evening or Sunday afternoon spent at Hatzic or Cultus Lake were enough to fill our memory banks with special family times. Perhaps it was those experiences that taught John to enjoy the little things in life.

One last photo from that vacation trip. Ernie, John, and I, in swimsuits, in the lake, each of us on an inflated inner tube. John, both hands free, is waving and grinning at the cameraman. Ernie and I cling, white-knuckled, to the sides of our tubes. That was when I learned to float. John taught me.

"Just hold your breath, put your face under the water, and lie on your stomach. No, no, no, don't let your feet touch the bottom."

I obeyed anxiously, my fear of his scorn greater than my fear of drowning. In later years, I watched as John stood in my backyard, leaning over my two-year-old son, Daniel. John taught him to make "motorboat" bubbles in his green Turtle Pool. Once more the circle closed.

Again, an undeniable irony. John had an incredible fear of drowning. It originated in his teenage years at Cultus Lake, where he nearly drowned. In spite of his fear, John took up scuba diving in adulthood. For a while he even worked on a fishing boat, diving for abalone. He faced his fears head-on, intentionally surrounding himself with them, until, at last, he covered his fears with his determination to control them.

All these memories, from pictures decades old.

6

Growing Apart

Today I pick up the photo album again. It has been many months since I have felt strong enough to do so. So many nightmares. So many sad memories I didn't want to face. I relinquished the photo album to the bottom shelf of the oak coffee table in my living room.

The weather today is a reflection of myself. This morning it was warm, though overcast. Around noon, dark clouds filled the sky. In midafternoon, the torrential rainstorm hit. By late afternoon, the rain had subsided and the dark clouds vanished. The sky filled with light, white clouds, which broke apart in the evening, revealing blue sky above.

My grief is so much like that. Ominous. Dark. Stormy. Then often it breaks apart, revealing a quiet light-heartedness.

Today I shall try again to look inside my houseful of memories. When last we left the pages of the album, John was ten years old. There is a gap. Then there he stands alone, looming over the photographer. He seems twelve or thirteen. His face looks stereotypically adolescent: cocky, trying to look older than he is, a veneer of toughness disguising the insecure, growing boy-man. He is wearing a checkered shirt and a brown vest, zipped up—symbolic of his life at that time. Unlike his looming appearance, John, at this age, stood apart and closed off from me and our family.

There are few pictures of this time in our relationship, at least photographic pictures. I do have plenty of mental images. I still see and feel and hear the silence between us then. It hurt. A wedge grew between us during John's preadolescent and teenaged years.

I see few pictures of connections now. I only feel the wind between us, as we pass each other in the barn after school, in the raspberry rows in summer. It persisted in the kitchen, the hall, and on the stairway leading to the dark basement, where John inhabited a bedroom in the furthest corner. The only words I heard him speak in those years were words he sang as loud music blasted out of his stereo: "Born to be wild, born to be free." And, of course, his conversations with his friend, our neighbor John.

Our foursome was no more. Ernie and I had been shed along the way—our once-shared interests were strewn along the road which now, instead of keeping us together, led in opposite directions. John's road was filled with his guitar and stereo, both vehicles for the loud and violent rock music that accompanied him wherever he went.

I stayed upstairs, practicing hymns and classical music on the piano in the living room. I tried to keep time to the beat in my head, a beat steadier and more predictable than the one shaking the floor beneath my feet.

Feet. John's feet carried him all over town at that age. Living on that dead-end road did, however, have one redeeming quality. Traffic on the 401 highway in those days was light. John could easily run across the freeway beneath the yellow-checkered sign at the end of our road. He arrived in town much faster than if he'd walked the long way around. He and his friend John would walk that street to Abbotsford, to a world beyond the world I knew, a world I discovered only through reports from others John had met while "out there."

The phone in our hallway rang late at night. "Who could that be?" my mother asked, alarm in her voice. Dad answered. The rest of us listened.

"Mr. Klassen?"

"Yes?" Dad didn't disguise his fear.

"This is the Matsqui police. We have your son down here. He and his friend were threatening to burn Moder's corner store."

"Oh," Dad said. He hung up, got his car keys, and drove to the station to pick up both Johns.

"We were just teasing," John said to Dad. "That man just doesn't like us, that's all."

Another phone call. This time, Mr. Quiring. "Mr. Klassen? Your son and his friends were throwing eggs and rocks at my son's truck. We'd like you to pay for the damages." It was Halloween.

"They drove by and threw water balloons at us first," John said this time. Dad only shook his head.

"They grow out of this stage," I overheard my father tell our pastor, when he visited our home. "They all have to go through this, but he'll grow out of it. They all do." My father's voice now sounded optimistic. I wonder if John ever knew my father said that. I hope so.

And then, John's freedom days arrived. He turned sixteen. Soon after came a set of keys to an orange Toyota Corolla. John no longer walked. He drove in style, music blaring from every opened window in that car. Now, for ten minutes every morning and afternoon, John's road and mine merged, as John became our chauffeur.

Each morning John dropped my brother Ernie and me off at the private high school we attended. He went to the public school on the other side of town. Those short silent trips to school and back home, are as fresh as yesterday in my memory.

We had little to say to each other. John attended public high school; I attended the private Christian school. John listened to Led Zeppelin; I sang in the high school choir. John partied on weekends; I roller-skated with our church youth group.

At home the silence continued, our only interaction the monosyllabic grunts and eye contacts made at the supper table, where we sat directly across from each other. "Pass the bread," or "pass the butter" were probably the longest sentences we exchanged.

I stared at John's face and arms, looking for signs of the John of old; John twitched under my scrutiny and glared at me, attempting to intimidate. It didn't work. For then, as now, I was my brother's keeper. I would save him from the claws of Satan, the lure of worldly fun. My prayers would keep John safe. "God," I prayed over and over at night, when I was safe in bed and John was out somewhere, "please bring John home safe tonight. . . . I'll do anything."

Then I'd lie awake, late at night and often into the early morning, until I heard the sound of his Toyota and saw its headlights bounce off my bedroom walls. "Thank you, thank you," I'd whisper into the cold, dark night. Once more my prayers had brought him home.

Yes, we were different. Or were we? I appeared to be the Christian one, while John had chosen worldly ways. I attended the Mennonite Educational Institute, sang in the church choir, attended Bible studies and youth functions, while John experimented with sin. In retrospect, I say he was braver than I was. Like him, I had many questions about life. I fled from my fears and questions by imitating others' faith. John forged ahead, seeking truth in his own way. He externalized his fears, his doubts, his questions.

He was honest. And I? Inside I longed to do the things he did. Inside I hurt as much as he did. My way appeared so safe, so "straight." But deep down I knew John's actions mirrored what I felt inside. Like a dentist's mirror, they revealed the cracks and rottenness my facade disguised.

No, we weren't really different; we only expressed our similarities differently. And that, I think, was a link in the chain which did finally connect us from childhood to his death.

"I always knew you were soul mates, you and John," one of his good friends told me recently. She was right, only it took me a long time to discover that.

There are a few actual photos of that time. In one, I'm standing between my brothers John and Ernie. I'm wearing a white dress. They're wearing suits. It is a special day. The three of us are getting baptized. We are publicly proclaiming our faith and officially joining the Mennonite church, where we grew up.

Though we still had many questions, it seemed natural that we should take this step in our faith journey. No, we didn't yet own all aspects of our faith, but our motives were honest, even if imitative.

There is something else significant in this picture. John's arm hangs around my shoulders. I'm standing stiff, unsure how to respond to this gesture of reconciliation. I, the "Christian," am afraid of my brother. I'm pulling away. I don't know how to communicate. We've grown too far apart.

Another picture. This painful one is filed in my head.

John is leaving for Ottawa to train as a radio operator. I'm crying in the kitchen. John hasn't said good-bye to me, his younger sister. I'm deeply hurt. He has left us all behind. He's on his own, traveling into the unknown.

I see myself standing by the kitchen sink, clinging to the counter top, weeping into a Kleenex, hoping I can conceal the redness in my eyes from the rest of the family. No one can see me like this. No one can know how much I love my brother, how much I want to talk to him, how much I hate this silence. *John, John, John, please come back,* I plead. *Please come back so I can say good-bye to you this time.*

The picture fades, the tears recede. There are happier times. The long distance phone calls. The visits home between his job training and his new employment on the weather ship, located off the west coast.

I made a special phone call to his weather station, a thousand miles across the ocean. "John, who do you think I should ask to my graduation?" I took his advice; I asked one of his friends.

"You're going out with Neufeld?" he asked, when he returned and found I was dating that friend, Walter.

The chain which had slackened between us began to tighten again. My new boyfriend held up the sagging links which hung between us. Then when John introduced us to his new friend, Tilly, another foursome was born.

The four of us grew together as we went on dates together. Hiking, swimming, then out for dinner, usually followed by walks afterward. And we talked. The tension remained, but now words finally passed between us. My brother was becoming more than just a brother. With our new friends and words, a friendship began to grow.

"What do you want from Mexico?" John asked.

"Oh, I don't know—anything. Well, actually, why don't

you bring me a silver charm for my bracelet?" I said, after a bit of thought.

A little silver Mexican hat is what he brought me. Today I wear that precious charm around my neck, for it is much more than just a bit of silver. It is a symbol of our friendship, of the care we felt for one another. Ours was a love not often expressed with words, but one which, like the silver that hat was made from, was malleable. It came in many different forms and gestures and, like silver, was precious.

The hat also symbolized who John was. Because his occupation was seasonal, he had many opportunities to travel. Mexico was one of his favorite spots. In one picture he is wearing a sombrero, and, indeed, could easily have been a native Mexican.

One last photo from our second decade. We're sitting on a large drainpipe beside a river in Hope, British Columbia. Again John is leaning back on me. But this time I'm not leaning away. We're smiling, he and I. No longer are we enemies; we're equals. And though we still have differences, they no longer separate us.

And so the third and final decade of our relationship begins. With friendship.

7

Brothers and Friends

The picture now in front of me is a happy one. It is my wedding day. John, in dark brown tuxedo, stands next to Walter, my grad date, now my husband. John is grinning, grinning, looking from me to Walter, shaking his head.

"This is my little sister Elsie," he seems to say with his eyes. There is undeniable pride mirrored by the look in my own eyes.

Then there was the sound of his voice when we returned from our honeymoon and he teased us about being married. And the countless times he called and said, "What are you guys doing? Would you like to come for dinner?"

It was New Year's Eve, our first together as a married couple. John and Tilly spent it with us. Together we waited for the clock to strike midnight. No, not in our living room. We were in John's airplane, flying over Vancouver.

"Happy New Year!" we shouted at 12:00 p.m. as we watched fireworks shooting up at us from the city below—an awesome and unforgettable sight.

We found a little house on Peardonville Road in Clearbrook which we purchased together. Walt and I lived in it; the rent we paid John covered his half of the mortgage. A few months later (a year after our wedding) John drove us to the Seattle airport. Walt and I were off to Europe for nine months.

The pictures of the next five years are mostly pictures John and Walter drew in the letters we sent between our changing addresses. Europe, Sweden, Clearbrook, Vancouver, Winnipeg, then Clearbrook again—these were the return addresses I used. I sent his letters to Alert Bay, Spring Island (population 15), Overlook Street in Prince Rupert, Zero Avenue in White Rock, and, finally, Aldergrove.

John's letters were always fun to read. In September 1978 he wrote to us in Europe. He was on Spring Island, a tiny island off the coast of British Columbia.

Here I am hard at work, finishing my last graveyard shift. My dog (man's best friend till he starts costing money) is lying quietly at my feet, doing his best to destroy a bone that he hunted down outside (lucky for the bone it's quite large). Anyway, picture this . . .

Beneath those words he had drawn a picture of himself, sitting at his radio equipment, his dog, Jonah Junior, at his feet. "Note the happy, tranquil expression on both the dog's and his master's face!" he wrote at the side. The letter went on to describe life on Spring Island. Nothing terribly exciting, but in John's words, a delight to read. It was a typical letter.

My words always seemed inadequate, and I don't recall much of what I wrote in my replies. But I do remember writing to him from Winnipeg, two years later. I was six months pregnant. "I'm supposed to feel fulfilled but all I feel is full and filled. . . ."

It was awkward coming home to British Columbia for Christmas that year, five months pregnant. I had always been skinny. Now I felt self-conscious. "Don't say anything," I warned John, as he approached me in our parents' basement.

He didn't. He smiled, hugged me, then lightly touched my stomach, a sign of approval.

Four months later, when we returned to Abbotsford for the summer, I introduced John to my new son. The love on John's face when he first laid eyes on Daniel needed no photograph; it's imprinted in my mind.

"He looks intelligent," said Tilly, as she, John, Walt, and I, stood looking down at the sleeping baby. Our foursome had now increased to what—a quintsome? John said nothing, just looked at Daniel for a long time.

There is the precious picture of the two of them that summer, when Daniel was four months old. John is smiling, a wide smile. His cheek presses against Daniel's cheek, where a dimple forms from Daniel's smile. They look alike—dark-haired, dark-skinned, and happy. Both are dressed in their best for my brother Ernie's wedding.

The bond those two formed that first summer of Daniel's life was strong. It endured through the next year when they connected only briefly at Christmas and the following Easter.

Then came the next summer, when I returned home to British Columbia for a rest. Walt's studies were taking most of his time, and parenting my active Daniel had taken its toll. I was exhausted. It was natural that I should phone John to pick me up at the airport.

"I desperately need a rest," I told him. He drove me to his house and took care of Daniel, while I slept and slept. In the morning, he walked to the grocery store and bought fresh bread for breakfast.

"How did you sleep?" he asked, when I woke to the smell of fresh coffee. "We didn't wake you last night, did we?"

"No," I lied, knowing how hard he was trying to give me a haven. I *had* heard loud voices.

In my photo album is a picture of that summer. John is kneeling on my parents' driveway, his arm around Daniel, who just turned one. Jonah, John's dog, is beside them. John is smiling. Daniel looks uncertain but stands close to his uncle. He clutches the slightly green apple Uncle John helped him find in my father's garden.

That visit was important to John and Daniel's relationship. Each was delighted with the other. Uncle John became a person Daniel learned to love and trust; his home, a place Daniel loved to visit.

My fatigue had been caused by more than Daniel's activity. Upon returning to Winnipeg, I discovered I was pregnant again. Eight months later, when I was almost ready to give birth, John phoned us in Winnipeg and offered to watch Daniel when I was in the hospital.

"Oh, John," I said. "I think we'll be okay. Some friends have offered to help." I was moved by his offer, even though it didn't work out—John got a flying job and had to leave. But that didn't matter. What mattered was the offer. It said we were friends.

Yes, our estrangement was ending. "My brother John" was now a phrase of pride. "My brother John is a pilot." "My brother John is such a character." "Daniel just loves my brother John. . . ."

The photo album was filled once more that spring after our second son, Matthew, was born and we moved back to British Columbia. We lived only twenty minutes from John. Phone calls became more frequent as long distance rates fell. "Uncle John" replaced "My brother John" as my children grew and related to their uncle.

Now John's presence loomed large in my life. Again the images. Daniel is sitting in the front of John's green VW station wagon, little suitcase at his feet, nose barely visible through the side window. He is just two but eagerly goes with Uncle John to spend the night.

John's home is not a place he fears. There is much to do at John's house, even though Uncle John has no children. He has a large back yard with a garden, a wooden helicopter, a fish tank to look at, a dog to play with, and Tilly, John's friend, to talk to. There is lots of love to make up for Uncle John's inexperience raising children.

"Daniel fell asleep sitting on the toilet," John told me, when I picked Daniel up.

"He what?" I asked.

"He fell asleep. I put him on the toilet, and when I came back he was sitting there, head nodding."

"What time was it?" I asked. This was not like my active Daniel!

"Oh, almost ten o'clock," John laughed.

"Ten o'clock? No wonder. That's two hours past his bedtime! What was he doing up so late?"

"Well, I kept asking him if he wanted to go to bed. He kept saying no. I thought he'd let me know when he was tired."

"John, John. How can a two-and-a-half-year-old know his bedtime?" Oh well, it didn't matter. What mattered was that Uncle John loved Daniel very much and Daniel loved Uncle John very much.

"Uncle John was so funny, Mom," Daniel told me after John had died. "He told me if I said, 'Huckleberry Pie, Huckleberry Pie, wake me up at six in the morning,' and then banged my head on the pillow three times, I'd always wake up at that time. And it really works, Mommy.

"I still remember going to Uncle John's house in Vancouver—you know, the one with the plastic-covered shed in the backyard."

"Yes, the greenhouse," I said.

"Yeah, he had vegetables growing there. And we had fish for supper. It had lots of tiny bones."

"Trout," I said, now also remembering.

"After that we played in the schoolyard across the street. I had on my T-shirt that said, 'My name's not Danny.' It got dirty. Do you remember, Mom?"

"Yes. I remember it well [the grease stains never came out of the T-shirt]. But you! How can you remember? You were barely three!"

"I don't know," Daniel said, with a shrug. "I remember lots of things." There was silence. Daniel sighed, a big sigh, then ended his verbal slide show with his usual, "Boy, I sure miss Uncle John; don't you, Mom?"

"Yes, Daniel, I do. Very much."

It was a difficult time, that time when John had moved from Aldergrove back to Vancouver. The relationship he was involved in was slowly disintegrating and the pain and stress was beginning to show. John's employment (agricultural aviation) took him out of the province for long periods of time in spring and summer. That absence didn't help cement the cracks in the relationship. In the fall of 1984, John and Tilly separated. We were all devastated. The foursome was gone again.

"Maybe you can help us get back together," John said, weak laughter following his words. I felt helpless.

"This is like a death," I told him.

"What do you mean? We're still friends," he replied, biting on his lower lip.

"It's not the same," I said and began to cry.

John left. He couldn't stand to watch my pain, the pain his own deep pain had caused.

"Uncle John must be lonely," Daniel often said to me after the breakup. "Why did they break up?"

My explanations of "sometimes things just don't work

out" and my own expressions of disappointment didn't satisfy. Two people he loved and cared for weren't together anymore. It didn't make sense, their "divorcement." Uncle John shouldn't have to be alone; he should have someone to care for him.

Both Daniel and Matthew loved having Uncle John around. "Why does Uncle John always have to go away?" and "When is Uncle John coming home again?" filled our household when John was away.

How heartbreaking to hear their words now: "Uncle John always went away. Then one day he never came back. I miss him so much."

How thankful I am for the relationship my brother had with my children! For in my mourning, in my remembering, they often (and usually to my surprise) give me additional pictures to remember my brother by. Their pictures are like gifts, for their memories are often so different than mine.

Take Christmas. John spent some of his last Christmases with us. I remember him on our couch, dressed in his new sweater and pants, Daniel and Matthew beside him. Daniel leans into John's chest and holds John's right hand. Matthew leans onto John's left shoulder and holds John's left hand. All three "boys" look relaxed, happy to be so close.

John had dropped by to wish us a Merry Christmas before spending the evening in Vancouver with friends. I still have the card he brought. It wasn't like him to bring a card, but the one he chose was so typically "John." It had an airplane on the front, spinning smoke designs in the sky. The pilot was smiling and waving. The caption above the picture read, "Spinning a little news for you," and then inside, "May this Christmas season bring you a big lift." John had added "spiritually!" in parentheses and beneath that, "John V.K."

It's odd how our memories differ. I remember John's coming. Daniel remembers his leaving. He always wanted John to say awhile longer.

Daniel also remembers John's Christmas tree in the little house he lived in, how bare it was compared to ours. "All he had on it were some candy canes and a few decorations, Mom," he told me. "But he let me eat some of the candy canes and chocolates." A momentary pause again and then, "Boy, Uncle John sure was nice, wasn't he Mom?"

"Yes, Daniel, he was."

Another picture. John has come for Christmas Eve. The boys are so excited to have him. They have bought him a transformer airplane.

"Hey, thanks!" he says. His hands fumble around with the robot, trying to convert it into an airplane.

"Here, Uncle John, " Daniel says. "I'll do it." He takes it from John. Sure enough, it's transformed in a minute. John coughs and begins to laugh.

"I still remember Uncle John sitting on the piano bench opening that present," Daniel recalled one day. "We gave him a transformer. Remember?"

"Yes, Daniel, I remember."

"Yeah, and I got a roadtrack for my cars," said Matthew.

"And I got blocks," said Daniel.

They are both right. And I got a silver chain and two books from Walt. John watched us open our gifts. "Thanks, " I told Walt as I put on the chain.

"Well, give him a kiss," John said.

The boys were in bed by this time. Both our parents had left. The three of us were alone in our living room now, sharing the few remaining minutes of Christmas Eve. John slouched lower and lower on the couch, until finally he was totally horizontal. His eyes closed as he dozed off. Walt and I sat silent a while, the only sounds in the room the cracking of the fire and John's rhythmic breathing. After a while we woke John. "Do you want to stay the night?" I asked.

"No, I'd better go home. I like my bed better," he said, then was off into the dark, cold night.

It was typical of John to visit at night. Sometimes he came in response to an invitation. Other times it was at his own whim. "Uncle John's here, Mom," the boys would shout, running to the front door. While I fixed dinner, John would talk to the boys in the living room.

"Hey Daniel, Matthew, come sit." He'd pat the place beside him. "What did you do in school?"

The boys would launch into their stories of how so-and-so had done this or that, followed by questions about John's day. It was a casual, natural conversation, one which usually ended with the boys and John wrestling on the floor. The meal was always spiked with, "Hey, Uncle John, guess what?" And no visit ever ended without lots of hugs and kisses for Uncle John.

Those were the planned evening visits. The unplanned, spontaneous calls occurred much later at night, usually after the children were already asleep. Then John came quietly. He would press his nose against the window in the front door. Sometimes he came to the large living room window, just a few feet away from where I usually sat on the couch, reading. John's giggle usually announced his arrival before his quiet knock.

"Whatcha doin'?" he'd say, and I'd reply, "Nothing much. Come in."

"Have you eaten?" I'd ask, anticipating his, "Got anything to eat?" I could count on John to eat our leftovers—good or bad. He wasn't fussy.

"Good banana cake, Els," he said, on one of his last visits. "Did you make it just for me?" he joked, knowing

I disliked spending time in the kitchen.

Those evenings we'd sit up late and talk. Often I got up and left John and Walt to finish the visit. Once he came so late only I was up, reading. "I came to say good-bye," he said, "I'm leaving for Ontario in the morning." It was 10:30 p.m. After a late supper, he was off into the night, his VW buzzing through the silent neighborhood.

Rarer still were his midday appearances. He'd fix his own lunch: deviled egg or ham sandwiches, a salad, leftover salmon, a muffin. Again, it didn't matter. I don't think he came for the food.

On one of those visits, I handed him one of my stories. "Oh, sick," he said after he had read it, then laughed at my sense of humor. He asked about the English literature class I was taking, then told me Tilly had a new boyfriend. Now his voice held no laughter.

No, John didn't come primarily for the food or even conversation. His hunger was far deeper than physical hunger; his words and laughter often came from a place far beneath his skin.

"Sometimes, when I'm filling out medical forms for the doctor for my annual check-up, I'm not sure what to mark for 'mental health,' " he said once. "Should I write, 'I feel blue sometimes,' or 'I had an uncle who committed suicide. . . .' " He laughed then, with his mouth. But his eyes betrayed him.

I want to learn from this picture. I want to hear beyond people's words and laughter. I want to respond to the feelings beneath. Most of all, I want to recognize that it is only because of John's deep pain that he could also laugh so deeply.

I have a lot of pictures, both tangible and not. I am rich, rich beyond measure to have so many images. But, as I recently heard someone say, "you can't hug pictures." Nor can they talk back. *I miss you, John; I love you, John. Can pictures hear?*

The back of my photo album is full of funeral pictures. There is his polished casket, wrapped in flowers. There is his body's final home, a hole in the ground, surrounded by people looking down, trying to comprehend. There I stand, white-faced but tearless—I'm too sad to cry today—staring vacantly at the winter-deadened grass.

"Well, I guess Uncle John must really miss his friends now, right Mommy?" Matthew announces loudly.

"Yes, I think he does," I reply, my voice as flat as the grass beneath the piles of dirt.

The album is full now, even though there remain some unfilled pages. John's life is over. No need to buy another roll of film on his account.

Today I start another album. Today a new life lies sleeping in my arms. I have a baby daughter: Rachel Johanna Neufeld. We chose the name *Rachel* because it means naive and innocent, which is how she came to us. And *Johanna*, the feminine version of John, which means "precious gift of God," in memory of my brother.

"We hope she will inherit his wonderful sense of humor, his warm and accepting love for people, and above all, the courage to be his own person," I wrote in her birth announcement cards.

Life and death. Full circle. The thread which separates the two is thin. John died; Rachel was born. I cannot say my daughter's name without remembering her uncle. Would I have embraced her unplanned life so tightly, so tenderly, without my brother's passing first? And would I cling so tightly to my memories were he still alive?

The door of life and death revolves. Get on, on one side, off on the other. Watch closely, though, for the same door leads to both sides. It's here; it's there. It begins; it ends. I have my pictures.

Mourning Bells Are Ringing

Hide and seek's over
death freed me of that
and I a writer
can't control the story.
The tear-wet hours.

—Audrey Poetker

8
Grieving

Grief. A painful word. Webster's dictionary defines it as "deep and poignant distress caused by or as if by bereavement." An inadequate definition, I think, now that I have lived inside this word.

It is impossible to completely define grief. Our English language is too limited. And grief is more than just a noun. It is a state of being.

Grief is being thrust into a black hole caused by an unexpected conflagration. Grief is as hard to define as the blackness in that hole. How does such blackness *feel*? Can you see, feel, touch, or taste it? You can't, of course, any more than you can grief. This is the closest analogy I can find.

It would be easier for me to *tell* how I grieved my brother's life and death. I could condense and interpret my grief experience: on that day I felt sad, yesterday I missed John, or today I cried. But like the attempt to define the term grief, it would be an incomplete picture of what I experienced.

So now I will share my most intimate writings—my

journal. I hope these words will *show* what I experienced and allow the reader to enter that experience with me.

I share my grief, not to sensationalize my experience, but only so others may also visit the house of grief where I and so many others have taken up temporary residence.

In Jewish tradition, persons in mourning were required to tear their clothes as an outward sign of grief. They were never to discard or exchange their apparel for a new outfit. But after a time they were allowed to sew the tears. The repaired seams had to be worn inside out, however, so all could see the frayed edges, the damage done by grief.

There was good in that tradition. Our society discourages displaying grief. Even the once traditional black "widow's clothing" is gone. The message is clear: Hide your pain.

Perhaps some of our traditions deserved to fade. But it's unfortunate they were not replaced with others. How can people in grief display their loss so others will recognize their behavior and responses as "normal"? Should they wear buttons on their clothes, or bumper stickers that say, "My son was killed," or "My spouse just died"?

Recently, I heard a woman tell how people responded to her after her son died of sudden infant death syndrome (SIDS). The woman was a clerk in a store. Many of her customers had seen her before and after her child's birth and had asked about the baby.

Now, her child dead, she returned to work. "How's the baby?" people asked. Her pain still great, she often couldn't respond. Sometimes she burst into tears. Sometimes she fled to the safety of the lunchroom. Sometimes she ignored the question. Her immediate impulse, she said, was always the same. She wanted to scream.

What should she do? The questions were not meant to hurt. But there was no symbol in place, no torn or black uniform to wear to tell her customers that her baby died.

I, too, have felt like her at times. Not because people asked about my brother, but because I didn't want to explain why I wasn't smiling much, or why I wasn't "fun" anymore.

I don't have an easy solution to this awkward problem, which we have created in our attempt to "ease" things for the mourner. But I do have my words, my thoughts, which I recorded along the way. They are my seams, turned inside out.

They're not nice to look at, these frayed, worn edges. But they have been a comfort; they have served me well. I wear them proudly, for they have helped shape a whole new me.

Now, two years later, a paradox: the seams are slowly fading. Not gone, not ever, but blending with the cloth around them. I wear my dress with pride, for I've survived. The hole is almost gone, the ground beneath my feet once more a solid piece of land. I've moved; the house of grief has been replaced by one of peace, which is my wish for all who have lived there. Here is my journey.

April 13, 1987

No answers. Just silence and grief. Grief is so difficult. I never would have imagined it to be so heavy and constant. Now, one month later, it is as intense as ever. But other things compete with it, and for some moments the pain seems to vanish, only to surface again.

Last Saturday, Walt and I were at Granville Market in Vancouver. I saw a tall, dark, mustached man. Instantly I thought of John. I thought how much John would have enjoyed being with us. I heard his laugh, saw his smile, saw his gait. And grief enveloped me.

I tried to swim free by concentrating on the musicians, but their German folksong *Das Leben geht vorbei* (life passes on) conspired with grief. I cried; we had to leave.

"There is no escape," I said to Walt. Not anywhere, anytime, ever. I wake and fall asleep thinking, *John, where are you? Why did you die?* I ache for myself, my parents, my children, my unborn child, John's many friends. Especially I ache for others whose companion also is now grief.

I feel oversensitized to suffering and death. Each time I hear a report of death on the news, it strikes me fresh. Another family is suffering.

I long for a sign from John that he's okay, he misses us, is sorry for causing this pain. *Where are you, John? Please tell me!*

I hurt so much when I think no John will eat at our table, no John will press his nose against my living room window, no John will sit on our couch. No John will ask for cake or a cookie or something sweet to eat with his coffee. No John will tell a joke, make fun of my ideas, throw my kids around, tickle them. No other "Uncle John" will ever replace this one. None. Ever.

GRIEVING FOR JOHN

Grief:
You are so cruel.
In a thousand ways you
wrap yourself around me,
a suffocating blanket of intensity.
You disguise yourself so neatly,
I hold you to my self,
not seeing your intent
until you strike—a knife

digging into my eyes,
my brain, my soul,
my guts.
In your tight grip I'm powerless;
no quilted warmth I find
beneath these tight-laced strings.
Your soldiers hold my fists at bay;
a pack of Fig Newtons,
the drone of airplanes overhead,
a song: Willie Nelson's
"You were always on my mind."
I wither, wilt, and crumble;
worship grief.
Held captive:
a prisoner of the past.

May 4, 1987

I have been dreaming the same dream all week. John is standing in the distance, beckoning me with his hand to come. I do not move. I stand riveted, terrified of going to him.

I wake terrified. I think the baby I am carrying will die at birth. I've told no one about the dream.

May 8, 1987

I'm so happy—I realize this is the first time since John's death that I actually *feel* something. I have a beautiful, healthy daughter, Rachel Johanna Neufeld. Life is beginning again.

June 1987

There is no escape. John is dead. I can't believe it. The newspaper confirms it. His empty house confirms it. His stereo in our house confirms it. His grave confirms it. His face smiles at me from the picture on my fridge door. I can't believe he's gone. Forever. The pain.

"Mommy, I'm glad and sad that Uncle John died. Number one: I'm sad because I miss him. Number two: I'm glad because now I got all his money from his piggy bank," Daniel told me.

■　■　■

Why, John? Why? Do you have any idea, any inkling of the grief you've left behind? Every day I wake and fall asleep thinking, *John's dead. John's dead. I can't believe it.*

Tonight we gather like vultures, dividing your money. *Your money!* What should we do with it? It's the last bit of *you.*

It makes me so mad! Who wants your money? Not me! Who deserves your money? It seems unfair to see your money distributed to people who will probably spend it differently than you. What would you have done with it? How can we buy things to remind us of you, to keep your memory alive for us and our children? Will you see what happens? And if so, will you be happy or sad? Your money, John, your money! Look down at us dreamers, Bruce Cockburn sings in the background.

Your grave. Cold. Ugly. Bare. Ironically, your "neighbor" is also John Klassen, born in 1897. He lived a long life. Was it as good as yours? Have you met him yet, this man who shares your name? How does it feel to be buried among those old people?

Music, oh, God, music. It pains me. Like a scalpel, it picks at wounds that have just begun to scab. Every note, every tune, hurts. It's you. You're in it.

My piano sits silent. I can't touch it. It hurts to play, burns my fingers, breaks my heart. Music, where is your joy, your comfort, your solace now? Do you still play guitar, John, or has a harp replaced it?

My couch. You're there, sitting in the north corner, laughing. Telling jokes. "Hey, Daniel. Come here. Tell me something." Now you're lying down.

"Elsie, you were born in the wrong place, in the wrong time," I hear you saying.

"Hey, John, you should read this book, *The Male Machine*," I say.

"Elsie, I've heard enough of this before. Got more coffee?"

■ ■ ■

"Mommy, I don't think you miss Uncle John much."

"How come?"

"You never cry anymore."

"I do, Daniel, I do. Every day I cry a little bit. I wish I could cry all day, but I can't. I have to do other things, too."

"Like what, Mommy? Like laugh at all the funny things Matthew and I do?"

"Yes, Daniel."

"Mommy, are you sad now?"

"Yes, Daniel. I'm very sad."

"I wish no one would ever have to die, Mommy."

"Me, too, Daniel."

"How much would you miss me if I died, Mommy?"

"Lots, Daniel, lots. My heart would break."

■ ■ ■

John, did you hear what Dad said on the way back from the cemetery? "I hope we don't have to go this way soon again, *denn bricht mein Herz ab*" (then my heart will be severed). John, take care of us. Please! Our hearts are breaking.

July 30, 1987

I'm sitting at my brother's grave. The sun has set, leaving behind a trail of first pink, then gray, and finally black clouds. A few pink streaks remain here and there—stragglers, remnants. Bruce Cockburn sings a song about the glorious hereafter.

I wonder. Can you hear me? Can you see me? Are you happy, John? I hope so. Have you seen all the tears with which we've flooded your grave?

August, 1987

All summer I've felt like two people. One lives inside my body, sitting at the controls. All day she tells the body what to do: when to rise, when to sleep, what to say, whom to say it to. She takes the children to the park, feeds the baby, entertains guests, talks to my husband, buys the groceries.

The other me floats high above, always watching, watching, watching. What will she do next, this person they say is me, this empty shell, performing her tasks like a robot?

"I am watching myself perform" I tell others seriously, but they laugh. I think I'm going crazy. I sit and sit away the minutes, hours, and days. Waiting, waiting, waiting. For what? I do not know. My grief-inflated self floats high above. John's death has fueled my flight.

"Eventually," say the countless books I read on death and mourning, "the pain will lessen. Your selves will merge again and you'll feel whole. Time will be your runway." I wait for fall.

September 10, 1987

I dreamed about John. The children were taking swimming lessons at an unfamiliar pool. I was waiting for Daniel in the lobby. He finally came out, walking toward me holding *John's* hand. John looked very, very real.

I was shocked. How could he be alive? He was killed in a car crash. I asked him, "How can you be alive?"

He said he had been unable to contact us to tell us it was all a terrible mistake. He wasn't killed.

He looked embarrassed. He also seemed aware of the pain he had caused everyone. And, in a curious way, he looked like he had absorbed all the pain we collectively felt.

I held him and hugged him and stroked his hair. It was so real. I woke filled with longing.

SEPTEMBER 21, 1987

Each time I visit you,
your grave,
I hear incessant buzzing.
Electric wires overhead send power,
life, to other places.
I raise my fist in anger, shouting, "Why?"
Why not here?
Here! Here! Here!
It's futile. Only silence,
cracked wide open by the buzzing current
flowing overhead, away from me.
All these noises overhead, and
I can't resurrect you.

Each time I visit you,
your grave,
I plot and plan ways to bring you
back to life.
I think, if only I could capture all these tears
that I and others leave behind,
then I'd unearth you

and inject them in your withered, shrunken corpse.
I'd rehydrate you
and gently graft my flesh onto your fire-blackened skin.
I'd blow life into your lungs and pump, pump, pump
your chest until your blood, renewed,
would shoot through your awakened veins again.

Each time I visit you,
your grave,
I say to you, "I'd do anything."
I would, you know,
for surely nothing hurts as much as this,
this pain of missing you.

October 15, 1987

Today the kids and I went to see your grave. I gathered bright yellow leaves while Daniel and Matthew ran around picking wild blue and yellow flowers.

Daniel cleaned your grave and said, "Oh, I miss Uncle John so much. Mom, I want to see him."

"I know," I said. "We all want to see him, but we can't. That's why it hurts so much when someone dies. But you know, I'm sure Uncle John can see us."

As we drove away, Matthew said, "Mom, once a long time ago, I thought of Uncle John at night and started crying."

Daniel was silent, then after a long time said, "Mom, I was crying for Uncle John just now, and some tears came out of my eye." I looked. Sure enough. His cheeks were wet.

Funny that in death John is present in our thoughts and conversations much more than he was in life.

It takes a long time, a whole lifetime, I think, to get used to a hole in your life. It takes a long time to accept that those stains the explosion left are permanent.

ON BROTHERS AND FIRE

I remember fires from my childhood—
the time I walked, barefooted,
on red-hot coals at our neighbors.
You took my hand and led me home.
I howled with pain.

Another time:
we poked long, thin wires into a fire,
swish, swished them in the sky,
painting the air around us.
Fascinating, until—
your red-hot brush came down
on my left arm.
It sizzled; left a blistered signature.

I remember fires at the iced-over pond's edge,
our snow-blown skating rink.
On late, dark, winter afternoons,
our faces turned toward the flames,
arms outstretched to dry our soggy mittens,
thaw our icy fingers.
Our toes, bound up in too-small skates,
flirted with the greedy flames.
They yearned for warmth, relief, release.

But best of all, I remember "garbage days,"
on Saturdays.
This weekly ritual of burning used-up things—
newspapers, Kleenexes, cardboard,
all things unrecyclable.
You and I stood stirring, poking,
prodding bits of garbage deep inside the flames
until, at last, the fuel was gone,
and all was gray-black ashes.

Brother, I remember well those fires,
But now this fascination turns to horror
as to my list of memorable fires,
I must add your last.

Your once-blue car, now slowly turning white
as high-rise flames lick off the paint
while you sit broken, huddled tight
against the melting circle.
Your flesh like hot wax dripping,
fingers fused into a lump of clay
Face and head and arms and chest
licked clean by hungry flames of fire.
Did you scream with pain, or
did you offer yourself, the new Elija?

Whom shall I send, John, to find you now,
a thousand firemen?
Could they retrieve you from your chariot of fire
which flew your soul away from earth?
I tell you brother,
fires have lost their fascination.

BOXING DAY 1987

I wonder why they call it Boxing Day?
it sounds so stupid.
Oh, now I know—
it means, put "Christmas" into boxes.
File it away on backroom darkened shelves
or corners high up in your closets.

This Boxing Day my brother's in a grave.
His box is nice; of oak and brass
with thick white satin lining—

a mattress for his decaying body.
The contents of his box,
no longer "John."
A pile of dust; a pile of useless compost.
How should we box away his life?

One little plot of dirt
is all he gets.
It measures six feet down,
three feet across.
No carpets here of red to hold
the footprints of his guests
who come and stand in slushy, melting snow
to say "hello," "goodbye," and
"how is Christmas this year, John?"
Ours has a bloody, gaping hole in it.
Sure wish you'd come and fix it all,
a kiss would make it better.

January 10, 1988

A life taken, a life given. What a year it's been. Yet I
don't feel abandoned by God. I have felt God's arms embrace me, stroke my head, assuage my fears, my guilt,
my struggles. I have heard God whisper, "Well done. I
see you're trying hard. And that, my child, is all I expect. I will supply the rest."

God's grace flows over me, healing, soothing, calming,
motivating me to press on, reach on, reach upward. And
then I rise again, to struggle on.

I have cried a lot this last year, more than all my
thirty years before, I'm sure, but so too I have learned to
laugh. I wonder—do laughter and tears originate in the
same place?

February 27, 1988

How well I remember John's last birthday, a year ago today. I stood knocking on his white front door, peeking through the white sheer curtains that covered the small window into the kitchen. I could see into the bedroom where John lay in his bed, still sleeping. It was 9:30 a.m.

I held a card in one hand, a pot of geraniums in the other. I laughed as I stood there knocking. *What an easy life this guy has!* For an instant, I wanted to exchange places with him, but then the reality, the loneliness of his singleness hit me.

His eyes opened, a grin formed, then he jumped out of bed, still rolled up in his blanket, and stumbled to open the door.

John shuffled around, fixing us breakfast—toast and coffee. The musty smell in the house was soon replaced by the aroma of freshly ground, brewing coffee.

While we were eating, my father arrived. He grinned at John as he shook his hand and said, "Happy birthday." I suddenly realized, after all these years, where John's grin originated.

John got out some old shortbread cookies and offered them to Dad. "I really shouldn't," he said, and took one.

I left, leaving the two of them together in that small kitchen.

I didn't know that the next time I came there with Dad it would be to an empty house, filled only with memories, John's ghost, and a box of stale shortbread cookies, sitting on that still-cluttered kitchen table.

Dad and I looked at it and both began to cry.

9

The Journey

One week before the first anniversary of John's death. It is a rainy, rainy day.

I picked up Daniel and his friend, Nicholas, from school. We drove up Gladwin Road hill. Already from the base of the hill I saw that there had been an accident. A northbound purple VW Beetle was smashed. For a moment I thought it was John—oh, God! Then a sharp pain.

We drove by. "The people weren't killed. They're just sitting in there. Look, Mom!" Daniel said.

He was right. The road was littered with bits of glass and plastic and a hubcap, but there was no blood, no fire. Just a broken but repairable car, and shattered nerves. They were lucky—this time.

Ten minutes later we drove by again, on our way home. As if sensing my thoughts, Daniel spoke up.

"Don't worry, Mom, no one's hurt. It's not our uncle."

He explained to his friend: "My uncle John used to have a car just like that Beetle, except it was blue. Remember, Nick? We used it in kindergarten?"

"Yes, I remember," replied Nick.

"Well, then he was driving—where was that Mom? Oh, yeah, to the United States, and he was in a car accident. A drunk driver hit him. His body got all smashed. You know how bad it was?"

"How bad?"

And then in a voice that was almost a whisper (I had to strain to hear), he said, "So badly we couldn't even see his face. There was nothing useful left."

"Oh."

"When we get home, I'll show you a picture of his car. His car exploded and burnt up. On the picture there is a fireman spraying the car. I think I know where the picture is. Wanna see it?"

"Okay."

Just another ordinary, rainy day. But the memory is as eternal as my flesh. And that, I think, is not all bad. Because sometimes I'm afraid of forgetting and thus losing John. But then a rainy day, a purple VW, and it all comes back. . . .

March 10, 1988

I'm on my way to Calgary to visit a friend. The boys are anxious about my going. Yesterday Daniel said, "Boy, it feels like you're going away like Uncle John always did. He always went away. Then he died. And then he had to go away forever. Mom, how come you have to go away?"

"Daniel, I don't have to. I want to. Just for a holiday."

"Well, I wish you wouldn't."

At lunch Matthew asked how many days I would be gone. "Three," I said. Counting on his fingers, he said he had thought it would be a lot more.

"Mom," he added, "is there a phone where your friend is?"

"Yes. Why?"

"Well, just in case I have to phone you."

"Matthew, it costs a lot of money to phone there."

"Okay. Well, where will you sleep?"

Then on the way to the airport Daniel again asked if we couldn't turn around and go back home. "I don't want you to go."

"Are you nervous about my going?" I asked.

"Why?"

"Because you keep talking about it and Uncle John. Don't worry, I'll come back."

"Well, why *did* he always go away?"

"Daniel, because of his work and because of holidays." For a few minutes the questions stopped.

"Mom, I'm really scared. What if the plane explodes and burns up? Please, can we go home?"

Matthew interjected now. "What if rain hits the plane? Will it explode?"

I felt sad and didn't know how to answer. Finally I said, "When it's 6:30 and dark outside, you'll know I've landed safely. If not, I'll call."

"Yeah, but how could your skeleton phone home?" Daniel asked.

I suggested he and Walt watch the news. Then he would know I was safe. That seemed to satisfy him. Until we got to the airport. Now tactics changed. Realizing I wasn't canceling my trip, they asked if I could change my stay to "two days instead of three."

It was hard going on that trip. But it was good for us to face the fear of separation, knowing that there was risk, that maybe I wouldn't return.

Hardest was this realization: John's death stole much more than his body. It also stole my children's innocence. They have learned too early the pain of separation.

March 16, 1988

Yesterday was the first anniversary of John's death. My busyness kept away my sadness. Today was a different story. I felt drawn to the cemetery today. *I can't even mourn spontaneously; I have to plan my time to mourn,* I thought with some resentment, as I packed my notebook and a snack for Rachel.

I stood and wept at the graveside. *This really isn't fair,* I thought. Flowers, birds, and sun communing in the background. Everywhere—life. And John was dead. It wasn't right.

When I turned to look at Rachel, she was grinning at me and playing peekaboo. I thought how much John would have enjoyed her. She is so wild, so full of life. I wish, I wish.

And I wondered about Joseph, the man responsible for John's death. How had he spent March 15? What had he remembered?

March 31, 1988

The day before Good Friday. The day before the anniversary of Christ's death.

Today is also Matthew's fifth birthday, a blessing in a way, as it calls me back to life. Even mourners must continue living.

So I began my day by remembering five years ago, when at 9:00 a.m. Matthew was born. Our second son, our ray of sunshine—born with a smile on his face.

"Happy birthday" I sang while dancing with Rachel. She grinned and yelled. Matthew hid his face in his hands and giggled. He was embarrassed.

"You're my special boy," I said, handing him his birthday present—a long-wanted jean jacket.

He hugged and kissed me. "Thanks, Mom, it fits perfectly." Such joy, such life. I was overwhelmed.

Later in the morning, we headed for the cemetery. As we drove up the long driveway to John's grave, I commented to the boys about the flowers. "Look at these daffodils. Isn't this beautiful?"

"Yeah," said Daniel. "But I sure wish Uncle John could come and take a quick peek at all the flowers. They sure are nice, aren't they, Mom?"

"Yes. And you know, I think Uncle John can see them."

"But how, Mom? He's dead and under the ground."

"Well, maybe he sees them with his new body."

"Maybe," replied the ever-skeptical Daniel.

As we approached John's gravesite, I was overwhelmed by the flowers surrounding John's tombstone. He would have appreciated the sight.

A yellow cluster of flowers crowned the tombstone, my mother's garden work. To the right of the stone was a large pot of browning daffodils, and ferns crowded close to a potted chrysanthemum. Another bunch of wilting daffs and a straw basket with red tulips and a cactus were below the stone. A note poked from between the plants. "All my love, John." The sender is from Toronto.

The note was addressed to John. But it also bore an unwritten message to those who came here: "See, I haven't forgotten," it said. I wondered how many other friends have not forgotten what this day was like a year ago.

And finally, to the left—a space. Here I placed my pot of brilliant pink azaleas. A sign of hope, of life. *I shall fill the spaces you have left behind, dear brother, with fragrant flowers I shall fill them.*

April 2, 1988

Woke up at 7:30, then drifted back to sleep until 8:30, finally crawled out of bed at 9:15. Walt asked if I had had dreams.

"Yes, nightmares actually. Why?"

Walt told me I was screaming in my sleep at 6:00 a.m.: "John!" and "I can't stop crying," and "I'm going to cry," and other indiscernible things.

Strange. Even though I woke knowing nightmares had filled my night, I couldn't remember them at all.

May 1988

SUNDAY AFTERNOON
AT THE CEMETERY

Tonight I'm having supper with my brother,
He's dead you know, for fourteen months already.
You think it's strange that I should come here
with my burger, fries, and chocolate shake?
Oh, yes, they're very salty.

People come and go, staying only briefly
staring, staring, staring at the tombstones
at their feet. What do they see?
Unfortunate, isn't it, that this isn't a cineplex theater?
Someone could get awfully rich.

A dozen chirpy robins hop between the graves,
Pick, pick, picking juicy worms
from beneath the blades of greening grass,
They're coming up for air, I think.
The earth below is heaving.

In the distance a young girl is jogging
"Run, girl, run," I shout.
"Feel the muscles in your legs;
embrace the wind.
Run, run, run as fast as you can."

My brother's grave is still and silent,
but flowers sprout and grow around his head.
A single robin feeds upon his plot,
then flies away, a song in its wake.
See? John is not dead.

June 12, 1988

Three more days until the fifteenth. Then it will be fifteen months. As I write, a plane flies overhead. Every small plane, especially if it's red and white, says "John is dead."

Last Sunday we were at Walt's mom's. It was a sunny day, so we were all outside. Matthew started yelling, "Hey, Uncle John. Hi, Uncle John. I'm down here. I miss you. Can you see me?" A small plane flew overhead.

Can you hear us, John? Can you see us? Are you riding on wings of planes, feeling the wind in your new face?

I know now that the only way to have nothing reminding me of John is to be dead. Much as I yearn to be rid of the painful reminders of John's death, my desire to live is not overshadowed.

But the living still hurts. Do I invite these memories, this pain? I don't think so. At least I'm not aware of it.

July 4, 1988

Oh, God! Murray just phoned to say his 21-year-old niece was killed yesterday in a head-on collision. How can this be? Just more pain. What's next?

I feel so helpless, so out of control. Are we, after all, just thrust into this life, with no control? Mere cogs in a wheel rolling down a steep decline? Do you care, God?

July 10, 1988

What a week. I've spent a lot of time at the Phillips'

house, just being there with them and helping as I could. I felt caught in a time warp much of the week; John's death and events surrounding it came crashing back. At times I felt unable to continue being their strength, but it *is* true that "in giving, we receive."

Still I feel so drained, so sad. This week has been a year long.

July 16, 1988

On vacation.

We're in Edmonton, with my second oldest brother, Henry. So much of what he does and says is like John. I cried in bed last night. I never thought this holiday would evoke such strong feelings and memories of John.

July 28, 1988

I'm aboard Alaska Airlines in Bellingham, on my way to Saint Paul, Minnesota, where I'll attend a conference on faith development. I didn't know the plane would be so small—only twenty seats. It's frightening.

As we sit on the runway for a few minutes, preparing for takeoff, I suddenly think of John. This was what he must have felt, a simultaneous rush of nervousness and excitement. "You feel close to God in church; I feel close to God in my plane," he used to tell us.

I can't help but think of the line from the anthem "The heavens are telling the glory of God." We are all silent as we take off, wrapped in our own thoughts. Our twenty streams of consciousness float about, filling the plane. All that energy! That alone should keep our plane aloft.

I'm determined to feel this flight as John might have. He was right. God is here, in the clouds which cushion and blanket this plane, in the ocean below, in the people around me, and in the snowy mountains to my left.

How can there be such beauty and no Creator? The beauty was put there to make the pain endurable, I see that now. The two must be inseparable. That is life: beauty, pain, love, and grace. It is enough.

July 30, 1988

"Out of the crucible of pain comes the promise of the resurrection." I am deeply moved. "And in the congregation is the face of God." These two thoughts, if nothing else, I shall take from this conference.

July 31, 1988

I've felt hugged by God this weekend. I came here with two expectations. I wanted affirmation that I was going in the right direction and new challenges for the future. I received both.

The worship services challenged me to face my pain with faith in resurrection. In sharing my faith journey with my small group, I received nonjudgmental space in which to be myself. I learned I wasn't alone. Others, too, had questions and doubts.

I discovered that the journey, not the destination, is the important thing. I received directions, warnings, possibilities, and grace to make mistakes. All these things were a picture of God, the body of Christ surrounding me.

I notice the fakes, the people who sound unauthentic, this weekend. You can spot them quickly. They're not real. They don't live inside their words. They use other people's words. All one such person could offer when I shared about John's death was "Yes, alcohol is endemic to our society." Such is life, I suppose. People everywhere just offering each other empty words. I feel sorry for such people. They need to learn how to economize their words.

Then home. Walt and the kids were at the airport. The kids were filthy and red-faced with sweat but so happy. Daniel clung to me and repeated, "I missed you, Mom."

Matthew was grinning. Rachel wasn't sure what to do. My wonderful family. I am so loved. I had forgotten how beautiful they all are.

August 1, 1988

This morning Matthew brought me breakfast in bed. I suddenly realized how in love with my family I am. Why can't it always be this way? But I guess the depths are what help us see the heights.

I keep thinking of a prayer someone read at the conference: "My ears are in love with hearing; my eyes are in love with seeing. . . ." I'm terrified. If I love too much, will I lose it? *Risks*, that's what it's all about, I learned this weekend. This is a risk, allowing myself to feel this way—but a good one, I think.

August 3, 1988

While visiting with friends tonight, I responded to the conversation with this comment "When one becomes intimate with pain, it becomes less frightening. I don't fear pain anymore."

I don't. I suddenly realize that.

Walt recounted how I had responded to a friend in grief this summer. He had been afraid to go along because "I didn't know what to do."

"But she was right," he added. "We had to be there."

Reciprocity—one person shares her pain, another his. And though the pain is collectively larger, it becomes, paradoxically, lighter. To be alone with pain is hell. To share it makes it bearable.

I'm humbled, in awe. How can there be such complexity and no Creator? Impossible!

August 6, 1988

If heaven starts here, then so must hell. Not having answers to a thousand questions is a hell of sorts. Is that the hell Christ descended into—not knowing why God wouldn't spare him pain and death?

Today I treated myself to three things: breakfast at VanEgmond's, yellow gladiolus, and three truffles. It was all good. There *has* to be beauty in pain and, if it is hard to find or there is none there, then one has to create it. So that's what I did today.

August 11, 1988

I think I've gone to heaven. We're on Saltspring Island. When we arrived yesterday I felt so overwhelmed.

"I only want to weep. I can't comprehend the beauty of all this," I said to Walt.

I sit and try to absorb, watching the water washing the rocks and sand, trying to make word pictures. I can't. I feel inadequate. If I lived here I wouldn't write another word. I'd just sit and stare.

I keep reminding myself that there is life beyond this bay. Back home, and elsewhere, there is pain. There is suffering, despair, hopelessness, and much need for love. This "paradise regained" will give me a reservoir of love and strength, so I can go back to the pain and those I've left behind.

Tonight I thought a lot about death and John. Where is he really? I wish I knew for certain.

August 16, 1988

Rain, rain, rain. God is crying, too. In some ways, I'm thankful for the rain. It makes it easier to leave. I'm tired, depressed, and so sad to leave this place.

August 19, 1988

Tonight we talked about the humanity of Christ and the image of God in people, about heaven and hell. I don't think God is so cruel that God will require people to relive their mistakes after death. I think it will be a fresh start, a clean slate.

August 20, 1988

Today I'm filled with hope and optimism. I'm full of determination to make the most out of my life and help others do the same. That is our calling. Not to answer all unanswerable questions, but to live fully, wholly, while still made of flesh. What comes after matters, but today is the important time. Today is the day we live within.

August 27, 1988

This week was bad. Thursday, driving home from the monastery, I saw the sun setting, just behind the pond. But I couldn't feel it. That scared me. I wanted to feel beauty but couldn't.

I drove home numb, not even the moon rising eerily behind the mountains evoked feeling. I went home and read *The Grieving Time: A Month by Month Account of Recovery*, by Anne M. Brooks. Finally, I can cry, especially when I read "Life gets easier, but it is never again easy!" Amen. I cry.

September 12, 1988

Last night was so bad. I felt so overwhelmed with grief and suffering. It seems that's all there is sometimes. I walked out of communion, to comfort someone else. Instead, I began crying and didn't know how to answer her questions: "Why doesn't God just stop it now?" and "Why are we here?"

"To help each other out," I said.

I do believe we need to help each other, but it's so hard. Life *is* difficult. But there is beauty in human connections, in love, in friendship. That's what we're here for, I think. I hope I'm right.

October 3, 1988

Some people might think it strange to visit the cemetery; I find great comfort there. Not that I imagine John to be there, but the John I knew, the body he inhabited while he was here, is buried there. I can't deny that. I don't want to deny that.

The cemetery where John is buried is not spectacular. It's a large field beneath a wide row of power lines. If you look south or west there is a busy freeway with a backdrop of industrial buildings. If you look north or east there are mountains, which in spring turn green; in fall, orange; and in winter, white. When I come here, I usually look down first, then up.

Beneath me is a rectangular piece of granite which bears John's name, his birth and death dates, and the words "Beloved son and brother." In the upper left corner is a plane flying over a tree-covered mountain. On the underside another inscription, "Under his wings I'm safely abiding." I always look up after I read that. John loved the sky.

Ironic, isn't it, that I come here because I need to remember he isn't here? So I come with daffodils and lilacs; with wildflowers, colored leaves, and evergreen branches. What else is left to do?

It is a painful place, this little plot of land he's inherited. Ironically, however, it's also a place of healing. I've watched my parents come here, seen my father wash the stone and clip the grass around it. I've seen my mother plant geraniums and tulips at the head of the stone and watched her place cut flowers from her garden into the jar she's pushed beneath the rich, wet soil.

Macabre? No. Healing. There is nothing left to say, nowhere left to visit him. Just here—this little piece of land in a field beneath the powerlines in the Hazelwood Mennonite Cemetery. I visit often.

October 10, 1988

Thanksgiving Day! What am I thankful for? It's difficult to find things this year; I have to strain. There have been two deaths this weekend. Three-year-old Kyler from my church, and a twenty-one-year-old student from the Bible school, Shayn Rempel.

I know I'm thankful for friendships, my family, my continued good health, my parents' well-being, my siblings.

I'm thankful for choice. In fact, I'll make a choice right now: to live, to live, to live! Today I shall go to the monastery and accept the love of God. I shall sit in the sunshine. I shall drink the beauty of the trees, leaves, lake, mountains, birds, chapel—all of it. It is God's arm extended to me. I am not alone. Everywhere God surrounds me.

I'm so thankful for that knowledge, for my faith in that. That is Thanksgiving!

October 12, 1988

It was a violent day today. I could hardly face it, I stayed in bed for 45 minutes after the alarm went off. Today I visited Anne and Rob, the parents of Kyler. Today I visited death, knocked willingly on it's door, and entered with those sitting on the mourning bench. I was afraid.

Before I went, I sat awhile, then played piano and wept. "Wounded, brokenhearted," I sang.

Tears helped a little. Truly they cushion our pain. I let them come, I invited them to come. I felt alone. I didn't want to visit; I'd rather hide at home.

But I had to go. Going gives meaning to John's death, which has taught me to reach out to other mourners. So I packed up my cards, my muffins, and stopped at the florist.

I hugged Anne, cried with her, told her my heart is breaking and my world has stopped for her this week. She seemed unbelievably strong; I'm afraid for her. I think she's still in shock.

Today I feel very small.

November 2, 1988

Two things I want to record. This morning as I stood outside with Daniel watching the pouring rain, I said, "Isn't rain neat?"

"Yeah, Mom, it is." He added, "But there's something I don't understand. How can the clouds hold all the rain inside them? I mean, you can put your hand right through the clouds, even when they're full of rain, but you can't feel it."

"You're right, Daniel," I said. "It's a mystery."

When I picked up Matthew from kindergarten several hours later, he and a classmate, Tannis, were debating who could run fastest.

"God can run the fastest of all," said Tannis.

"No," replied Matthew. "There's no room to run in heaven. It's far too crowded up there with all those people."

Perhaps the rain that fills the clouds is actually the tears of those in heaven. Perhaps they miss us too.

This afternoon there are two funerals that I know of. The first is for an older woman who had Alzheimer's disease for fifteen years. She spent her last ten years in a mental institution.

The second, baby William, was born last Monday, two months premature. He died Saturday, an undeveloped person who never left the intensive care nursery. He never felt rain on his face, mud in his hands, grass between his toes.

But he lived to feel his parents' kisses. He lived to feel their warm hands and the gentle strength of their arms, wrapped around his fragile, incomplete body. I wonder— do the scalding tears that fell on his face now seed the clouds dropping their burden on his tiny grave? I long to know the answers.

November 4, 1988
An open letter to God.

God, I feel like screaming. I feel worn out. I feel tired. I feel discouraged. I feel hopeless. Everywhere I turn there is more hurt, pain, sorrow.

My brother is dead, my kids are noisy, Daniel cheated in school today. Rachel shrieks all day, my cousin Anita is dying, two children have died in our church in the last three weeks. I can't take it.

I've tried to keep up with things and that has helped a bit. But it hasn't cured anyone's cancer or brought back the dead. I just don't know. I feel so discouraged.

December 5, 1988
The boys and I were sitting in front of the fire. Daniel and Matthew were discussing Uncle John and how he must have looked after the car crash. Both of them were trying to elicit details from me. I tried to explain that he was very smashed. Finally, in desperation, I pointed to Matthew's fingernail (injured when he inserted it into the chain on the exercise bicycle) and said it was like that.

Daniel was quiet a moment. Then we discussed how John had a new body now and was still alive. And even though we couldn't see him, we could keep him alive by talking about him. "The memories keep him alive in our hearts," I said.

"Heaven is in our hearts, right, Mom?" said Matthew. "I used to think it was up there [he pointed up] but now I know it's here," he said, pointing at his chest.

"You're right, Matthew," I said. Several months earlier Matthew had decided that "a bit of heaven is right here" because "God lives in heaven and God is here beside me," so heaven must be, too.

"And Uncle John lives in my heart," he said.

December 24, 1988

Before going to my family gathering today, I drove to the cemetery. The caretaker was hunched over a tombstone with a scrub brush and a pail of water. He was cleaning up the cemetery for all the extra Christmas visitors, no doubt.

At the top of the driveway I parked the van and pulled out the things I had bought earlier—a grapevine wreath, a plastic green leaf with holly berries on it, and a bird's nest with a white dove in it. The bird had one real feather on each of its wings. It was surrounded by miniature gifts and candy canes.

I placed the decorated wreath against the gray stone at the head of John's grave. From the van came the sound of Rachel's screams. "Merry Christmas, John." I said quietly.

December 26, 1988

"Oh, I wish Uncle John were alive; I have so much to tell him," Daniel said today.

"Maybe you can find someone else to tell."

"No," he said, "it's not the same."

"Well," I said, "you can tell him in your head."

"No," he said, irate now. "I want to see him."

How I wish I could grant my child this Christmas wish! Seeing his pain is worse than carrying my own. I wish Santa Claus were real.

February 25, 1989

Last night two young students from the Bible college were killed in an automobile accident. As I reflect on their deaths, I can't help thinking about the book I'm reading, *What Was Good About Today?* It's the story of a nine-year-old girl, Sara, who died of leukemia. Sara was exceptionally brave.

Only once in the story does she feel defeated. She bangs her head against the wall, screaming. When her mother finally calms her, Sara explains. A little boy had just been admitted. He, too, had leukemia.

"It's all so sad, it's just all so sad," she repeated over and over to her mother. "This is just the beginning for him," she said.

That's how I feel today. This is all so sad. Today is the beginning of a terrible journey for two more families. I wish to scream for them, too.

February 26, 1989

Today in Sunday school, Daniel asked his teacher, "What's the point in celebrating someone's birthday if that person's dead?"

"Well," his teacher wisely replied, "you don't exactly have to celebrate, but you can remember how it was on his other birthdays."

Tomorrow is John's birthday.

February 27, 1989

I woke and wondered how I ought to feel today. I've healed a lot. I don't feel overwhelmed with sadness. I just remember fondly John's past birthdays.

In the evening, James, the boys' twenty-one-year-old friend, came to visit. He had just returned from a six-month trip to Australia. The boys were ecstatic to see him. Daniel looked up at James, his face glowing. I yearned to be more powerful. If only I could bring John back. I wish, I wish.

"Mom, I think James is dead. I don't think he's coming back, do you? He's been gone so long, I can't believe he's coming back," Daniel had told me, just a month ago.

"Oh Daniel," I had assured him, "he really isn't dead. He'll come back soon."

Now James *was* back and Daniel's eyes danced like I've never seen. If only James were John.

March 8, 1989

Today will be the last entry. My grief isn't over. But I accept that it will *never* be over. A week from today will mark the second anniversary of John's death.

Two years. It has been a long journey. But I can see today how far I've come. Is it over now? I don't think so, but it has become easier. The feelings still come, and I still miss John. But the constancy of grief has gone.

I *am* getting better. Smiles come quicker now. Laughter rings authentically. Nights are more restful. Grief is no longer a word I merely toss around. Now I hold it gently and with awe.

Sometimes, I feel guilty for not thinking about John as often as I used to, for not crying as much as I used to. Even my journal entries refer to him less and less. But there comes a time to move out of grief and loss, and turn to what is left in life.

John had thirty-two years of life but only one death. To focus only on his death would dishonor his life. I can learn more from his life than his death.

And so I turn toward my life, a life I wish to live in

the influence of John's life, not only his death. I've learned much from grief. To cry, to feel more deeply, to care, but most of all to live.

A friend, after reading this section, wrote a poem. He too, has experienced grief. He, like me, has found hands of hope when drowning. I'm thankful for the hands. His poem mirrors my own thoughts.

BLACKNESS: REFLECTIONS ON READING A FRIEND'S JOURNAL

Stabbed by blackness, not by light,
Grief—my companion
snuffs the light—
blankets all.
Not like the gathering twilight,
the graying forms assemble;
not a dimming, but a stabbing;
not a fading, but a
sudden groping for light,
for forms, for hands.

Through the days—or
were there days?
The darkness marched
to different meters.
No minutes, no hours
marked the passing time.

Clocks suspended in
time and space.
Blackened hands on blackened
face—may have moved,
but no one saw.

The blackness blackened,
the grief persisted,
pushing me down the
chasm of pain.
No bottom, no sides,
No starry sky,
All blackened without form
and void.
Darkness covered the earth.

No guiding light,
no Polaris north,
to set a mark.
I drifted—I wallowed
on waveless seas,
abandoned by time
and friends alike.
Only grief, my companion,
kept vigil on my darkened heart.
I cannot tell the start—
the place where time
began to tick and tock.
I only know—I felt.
Awareness came—a
silent scarred and blackened hand
slipped into mine.
A comrade joined the darkened space.

The walls returned,
the floor arose.
And darkened forms
their shape renewed.
And forms reshaped
and colors hued.
Deeper in eyes renewed

perspective changed—
the hand remained—sight
returned, but not the same.
For even blackness gained a
hue and color it became.

—Murray E. Phillips

Life on this side of grief will never be the same. But I do admit the new and different me is better. Nothing looks and feels and tastes the same; it shouldn't. John is dead. I'll always grieve.

Who Is My Neighbor?

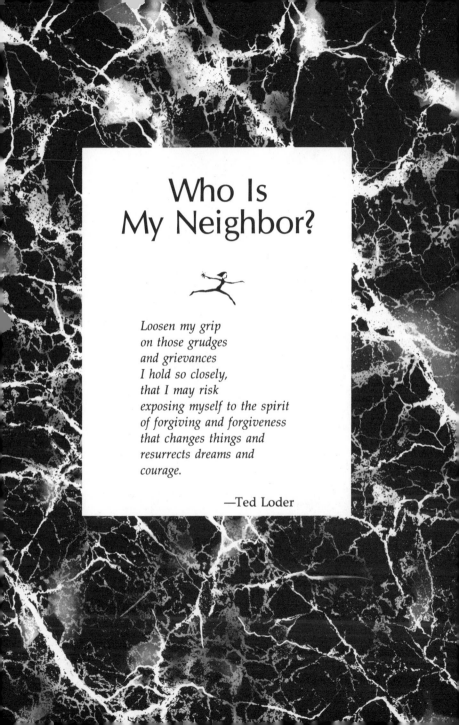

Loosen my grip
on those grudges
and grievances
I hold so closely,
that I may risk
exposing myself to the spirit
of forgiving and forgiveness
that changes things and
resurrects dreams and
courage.

—Ted Loder

10
Facing
My Neighbor

A sudden death is a horrific event. A sudden death which could have been prevented is even worse. There is no comfort in the thought that a body stopped living because the heart or lungs malfunctioned, nor is there an element of nature to direct your anger at. There is always only this thought: another person caused my brother's death. And that is no comfort. That is only a catalyst for anger, blame, and bitterness—which may lead to thoughts of murder and retaliation.

Such was John's death. It was hard enough to accept his sudden death at his young age. The fact that a man John's own age caused John's death only intensified my grief. For a long time I referred to that man, Joseph, as a "murderer." Today I can no longer call him murderer. Now I call him either "the man responsible for John's death" or "my neighbor's stepson."

Discovering that Joseph is my neighbor usually leaves people speechless. Certainly I was shocked when I first discovered this. But now I realize that, in a sense, I'm fortunate to live so close to Joseph, for the closeness has stirred healing. Our proximity has forced me to face him and what he did.

From the beginning, I wanted to meet the man responsible for the accident. Like other members of my family, I was angry. But I felt I must exercise my faith even in the context of this horrible event.

"We're pacifists," I told my husband over and over. "We have to respond as such."

My journey has been lonely. I realized early that each person in our family struggled in unique ways with feelings towards Joseph. For some it wasn't an issue. They simply dismissed it as an "accident." Others felt and verbalized their anger with such intensity that it frightened me. Still others could not, or chose not to, verbalize anger. I recognize the validity and process of each person's journey. But the journey I chose was my own. I alone had to walk it.

"How do you feel about Joseph? Angry?" was a question people asked, shortly after the accident.

"Well, actually, I'm surprised," I would reply. "I don't really feel angry, just incredibly sad. Sad that everyone's lives have been so hurt."

In retrospect, I have to admit I was angry, only I didn't explode like others around me. Their anger terrified me, for it exposed their dark sides. I didn't want to show my dark self at first. Yet as time went by, my own anger did surface. I had yet to learn that there is nothing wrong with anger itself; it's what you do with the angry feelings that matters. I had a right to be angry, my parents had a right to be angry, my siblings and John's friends all had a right to be angry.

"If we give him our anger, we'll give him more than he has already taken from us," I told my father one day, when we were discussing the accident.

"He has stolen his way into our lives," my father

replied, his fists clenched on the kitchen table.

"Yes. But, Dad, if we stay angry, he'll stay in our lives even longer and keep taking more from us. John is dead. He won't come back. Let's not give away anything else," I replied so casually, so self-righteously.

My father was right. Joseph had entered our lives. I hadn't yet accepted that, to defuse my anger, I'd have to admit and claim its presence. It would take awhile.

I can't recount the time—the seconds, minutes, hours, days, and months—I've spent dealing with my brother's "murderer." I'm thankful I kept a record of some of those times. I kept a journal. I wrote letters to friends and acquaintances. I wrote several stories in which my feelings finally surfaced.

Now, almost two years later, I can see the progression. I can see the pain, the frustration, the agony—and the victories. And I can say it was worth it. I'm glad I chose to walk the path I did.

I'd like to share some of my records with you. Not to boast, but to inspire others in a similar situation to choose also to walk Christ's path.

Several weeks after John's death, I read an article in *The Mennonite Reporter*, a religious newspaper. The author, Wilma Derksen, a journalist for the paper, told the story of her daughter's murder.

Candace had been kidnapped on the way home from school, raped, murdered, and left in an abandoned shed near her home. The murderer hadn't been found. What impressed me was Wilma's decision to walk the path of forgiveness. She recognized how sick this person must be and how much he needed the love, forgiveness, and grace of God.

I was stunned. Here was a person whose daughter had died in a heinous manner. Yet she was choosing to heal by seeking to forgive! I clipped the article. Though I filed it away, I couldn't put the story out of my mind. A question began throbbing in my head: Should I try to face my brother's murderer?

I think what also inspired me to choose this path was seeing anger's effects on some of my family members. Threats of legal suits and "making him pay" depressed me. I found it difficult to believe this would be a road to justice and healing.

I believe Wilma's article was a godsend. It showed me Christ incarnate, the Christ of the New Testament, alive and working in 1987. Most important, Wilma was a human version of Christ. Wilma didn't describe an easy journey. Her response didn't flow from one evening of prayer. It came after and in the midst of anguished prayers. Wilma painted a realistic picture, an evolving picture, a process. That made it seem possible for me to try a similar route.

When you experience a sudden, preventable death such as John's, you need healing. Healing is what the grieving person wants and longs for first—then justice. But I believe justice can only be requested in the midst of healing, for it is only then that one can again see life as it really is.

Looking at the world through angry eyes presents a distorted picture. You see only evil present in your own desire to seek revenge for a death that should not have happened. ". . . eye for eye, tooth for tooth . . ." (Exod. 21:23, NIV). You forget love—the love you shared with the person now dead and the love even the person responsible for the death deserves. And you forget so easily (yes, even the Christian, and, sometimes, especially the Christian) the unconditional and ever-present love of Christ.

Yes, healing is what the wounded person needs most. That, I think, is what ultimately motivated me to face the man responsible for John's death.

I was seven months pregnant when my brother died. Sometimes I think that profoundly affected my response. I was so concerned with damaging the baby that I deliberately delayed a lot of my negative feelings. *After the baby is born*, I thought, whenever strong feelings bubbled.

Now I think the pregnancy was a type of grace, because it gave me time. Time does, in itself, grant healing, even if only a superficial one. The deep feelings must be faced and named for wholeness to occur. But, paradoxically, that again requires time, time in which other persons and events can cross your path. If you're fortunate, time will bring these at precisely the ripe moment.

My pregnancy gave me time, time in which I chose not to ask big questions about getting even with my brother's murderer.

Instead, I wondered who he was and what he looked like. At times I even wondered what he was feeling. Did he have any remorse? But mostly I began absorbing clues I got from the newspapers and gossip from people around me.

I learned that the man who killed my brother was named Joseph. He was John's age. He was divorced. He had two children who lived in Alberta, from where he had moved a year ago. All trivia, I thought. Only one thing indicated remorse; the policeman said Joseph broke down and cried after being told John was dead.

At last, something I could cling to. Joseph must be human, after all. He must be more than an evil force which killed my brother.

In June, three months after John's death, the police finally charged Joseph. The three counts were impaired driving, impaired driving causing death, and dangerous driving causing death. Joseph could now enter his plea.

A date was set for the end of June.

I decided to attend. Now there were no excuses left, no reason to postpone the larger questions. Rachel had been born. Now the only body I needed to take responsibility for was my own. I needed to see the man.

It was a warm, sunny day when I walked over to the courthouse. Rachel was strapped to my chest in her Snugli. I entered the room feeling detached. Was this really happening? I stroked Rachel's head as I sat in that room, looking around for a person who might look the part.

"That must be him," I said to my sister and brother. I pointed to a long-haired youth sitting in the front. His stringy hair covered his ears, but I could still see the earring in his left lobe. He wore jeans and a jean vest, a black shirt, and big cowboy boots. He looked like a criminal.

I was wrong. That man was being charged with shoplifting. I kept looking. Each time I thought I had found the man, he would stand in response to a different name.

Then finally Joseph's name was called. The door opened. Joseph walked in, a cleanly dressed, nice-looking young man. I was stunned. This was not what I had expected. He could have been my brother. Dark hair, moustache, brown eyes. Uncanny!

"How do you plead, Joseph?" the judge asked.

"I haven't had time to find a lawyer yet, Your Honor," he replied. He asked for a new date to enter his plea.

I couldn't believe it. Worse, the judge accepted his request. His plea was postponed to July 15. Joseph walked away. Marg and Ernie, my siblings, sat riveted, stunned as I was.

I jumped up and followed Joseph. "I'm going to talk to him," I told the others.

Later that evening I wrote in my journal:

Oh, God! I saw him face-to-face. I intended to say, "Hey, Joseph, how do you sleep at night?" in a mean, sarcastic voice. But I couldn't. We stood there, our eyes meeting.

I said instead, "I'm John's sister, and I just want to know how you feel about all of this. I want to know your side." Where those words came from, I'll never know. They didn't originate with me.

His eyes looked so sad, so lifeless, as though he looked but didn't see. His face paled. "It wasn't my fault," he said quietly.

"Don't you think your being drunk had anything to do with it?" I tossed the words at him. He threw them back, rearranged.

"I wasn't drunk."

"The Breathalyzer lied?"

"No, but I only had a few drinks."

The ball was in my court again. I threw it back with full force. "If you have any remorse or feel at all bad, the least you could do is write my parents a letter and apologize. You have no idea what this has done to them and us. You just can't imagine."

The two women with him moved close. He looked agonized, his face twisted.

"What's their address?" I heard one of them ask.

I dug in my purse for paper and a pen and thrust them in her direction.

"It wasn't his fault," the dark-haired woman said. She took down the address.

"It always happens to the nice guys," said the blonde one.

"It doesn't matter," I said. "A life has been taken."

I looked at Joseph again and said, "I hope you never drink and drive again, because the next time you could kill me—or you," I said, pointing to the blonde. "Please write my parents," I said again, then walked away.

My head and heart were pounding. I felt strange. Mixed feelings. Glad to have a face in mind and not some evil force. Glad to see there seemed to be remorse. Incredibly sad that so many lives had been tainted. Amazed at my reaction when coming face-to-face with Joseph.

Still left with some desire to dig a knife into his pain, inflicting more pain, guilt. *Suffer, suffer, Joseph. Still you can't possibly suffer as much as we. Feeling guilty yet? No? Dig deeper! Can't sleep? Good. Neither can we.*

Then I remember those eyes. Painful, sad, hard-to-carry-on-with-life eyes. A part of me is glad he hurts. That helps a tiny bit. But it doesn't bring back John.

What is justice? How can I forgive? And if I forgive, does that mean he shouldn't be punished? How much is a life worth, anyway?

I thought I had faced my feelings when I faced Joseph that day. I thought I could truly love and forgive him now. I was wrong.

A few weeks later I met Wilma Derksen (the woman whose article I had read). She spoke in our church about her experience. I was deeply moved. When she finished, she asked if there were questions.

"If your daughter's murderer is ever found, what would be a just punishment?" I blurted out, from the back of the room. My question stunned me. I began crying.

"Well," replied Wilma slowly, "I think for me true justice might occur if I could have my daughter back. But that can never happen. . . ."

Afterwards I stayed behind and Wilma hugged me. "What's wrong, what has happened?" she said.

I told her. I said I too wanted to forgive. "Can I write to you?" I asked.

"Sure. And maybe we could meet for coffee before I go back to Winnipeg."

We didn't meet again, but I did write. I started my first letter that same July afternoon. "Dear Wilma, My heart is breaking. For you. For me. For all of us who have lost loved ones at the hand of someone who made a bad choice. . . ."

I wrote of John's accident, my feelings, meeting Joseph in the courthouse, and how I sensed the pain in his eyes. And I wondered again, "What is justice?" It was a long letter. Though I finished it on the afternoon of meeting Wilma, I didn't mail it until August 14, 1987.

I attached this to the front.

> I wrote the following letter to you on the same day I met you and intended to get in touch with you while you were still in B.C. But that never materialized.
>
> I ask myself why, and I realize I am afraid. The day after I saw you and wrote the letter I was in a restaurant with a friend when Joseph, the man responsible for John's death, walked past and sat behind us.
>
> I felt physically ill. My head was spinning, and I felt an urgent need to vomit. My reaction surprised me. I thought by confronting him at the courthouse I had somehow purged myself of him. I was wrong.
>
> I realize this will always haunt me. That seems difficult, but somehow this realization eases the difficulty in that I at least will expect such feelings. I would like to continue corresponding with you. . . .

Wilma's reply was prompt and encouraging. The fear I had expressed of meeting with her, she said, was understandable. "I'm still afraid of meeting those who have gone through tragedy. I think it's because they remind me of my own pain and refresh it."

Wilma had hit the nail on the head. Had I met with

her, I would have verbalized my pain, my anger. My fear, I think, was not so much of her as of myself, my own feelings. To have her identify with those feelings was freeing to me. No longer did I feel so alone.

Wilma also freed me in another way. She not only validated my fears and anger. She warned me of what I could expect on my quest for forgiveness.

> I guess what I realized again when I was reading your story was the need to process the whole event over and over. And it seems that I always start from the base of anger, questions with no answers, and then move on to acceptance and peace.
>
> When I've reached this stage, I think I've made it. But the next day or next event—and I have to go through the whole process again. I'm beginning to think there is no way around this. We're human and we're going to react to loss with anger.

Then these words of encouragement:

> What makes a believer in Christ different is that we know the path. We know that we can be angry. We can ask God "Why?" But we also know God expects us to forgive, to try and understand the offender, to realize that we can make mistakes, too. God expects us to realize the depravity of those who don't know Christ and because of this turn to violence—or, in your case, drinking—to escape their pain.
>
> The path continues on to saying, "Your will be done." We move to thanksgiving. Not for the sin, but for God's redeeming power and love that surrounds us. And then to a new surge of energy to do something about the evil in this world and hopefully spare others from going through the pain we've faced.

Wilma ended with these words. I pray that you'll continue your struggle against bitterness.

Bitterness? I thought. I wasn't bitter, was I? Hadn't I made an effort to understand Joseph when I approached him at the courthouse? I thought I was already loving and forgiving him by that gesture.

Soon after Wilma's letter came I wrote this in my journal: "I can't believe this! Joseph lives next door! I've known this for two weeks but have ignored what I saw, hoping it wasn't true and would go away. It didn't."

First I noticed a white car parked next door which resembled "the car." Then Daniel came running home one day saying that "the car in Cast's yard killed somebody." Jamie, a neighbor boy, had told him.

I walked past Cast's yard and knew then that Joseph must be there. How? I have no idea. I just knew. But I put it out of my mind. I didn't wish to know.

On Saturday I was home alone with Rachel when Margaret, my sister, called.

"Do you know what's going on at your neighbor's?"

"What do you mean?"

"Well, how well do you know them, the ones to the north of you?"

"I know their first names. We talk over the fence. You know—superficial talk. Why? Are you interested in buying their tent trailer?" I asked.

"No," she said and laughed a strange laugh. "I just drove by there. Guess who's there?"

"I know," I said. "I saw him a couple of weeks ago. But I literally put it out of my mind."

"I feel like going over there and asking him when he's going to write Mom and Dad that letter," she said. "I just felt sick when I saw him."

"I know. I felt the same way when I saw him. I just haven't wanted to face it."

We talked more, but I couldn't concentrate. Then I went outside. Although it was a hot day, I was shivering. I went back inside and put on a jacket, then stood in the backyard staring into the neighbor's yard. I could see the car on the driveway, its doors open and a bucket of water beside it.

I was shaking so badly. I felt just like the night John died.

"What are you asking of me?" I heard myself say. In that instant I knew that again I must talk to this person. One thought entered my mind and repeated itself: The way of God is difficult but that is the way I have chosen. This is what I must do.

I walked down the road and stood behind the tall shrub on Cast's front lawn. Then I saw him approaching his car. I was filled with anger. *How dare he be alive?* I thought, *Look at him in his red shorts and tanned body, look at his muscular legs and bare feet.*

I thought of John and what had happened to his once strong and beautiful body. "It isn't fair!" I cried to God.

Then I remembered my neighborhood when we were children. John was always the first to meet the new neighbors. I paced back and forth, went home, then came back again. This time I forced myself to walk up that driveway.

He saw me. His expression didn't alter. I wondered if he recognized me.

"Well," I said, "irony of ironies. Are you living here?"

"Just a few more days," he said. He didn't look into my face.

"I can't believe it. What a life," I said. "Did you know we lived next door?"

"I just found out a few weeks ago."

"Is Cast your father?" I had no script to follow.

"No, my stepfather."

"You know," I said, "I look at that car and I just want to smash it to bits."

"It's not the car."

"It looks just like it. What did you do with the other one, sell it?"

"No, it was totaled."

"You know," I said, "I have to come and talk to you so I don't hate you. I don't want to hate you."

Silence followed.

"You know," I said again, "I'm glad it was you and not John who did this. It would have been hell for him to go through this, to live with doing something like this."

"Yeah, well, there's nothing I can do about it now." His tone was flat.

Silence again.

"So, how are you doing? Are you working?" I could hardly hear my voice.

"Yeah, at the Blueberry Co-op."

"Someone said you knew John. Did you?"

"No, but he did some spraying for us. I've only been here a year. It's a small town though, and getting smaller all the time." He looked down again.

"I have to do this, you know. I have to come and see you so I don't hate you. I want you to know that our family will never do anything to you. You don't have to worry about that."

I started to leave.

"Well, take care of yourself," he said, as I walked away.

I wanted to scream, to let loose all my emotions, but I didn't. "The cost is very high, God, very high," I heard my voice say.

I went inside, picked up Rachel, and drove to the cemetery. I knelt at John's grave and wept.

"Did I do the right thing, John? What would you have done?" I asked. "Somehow it feels right. But I don't know. I don't know."

John loved people, accepted them. I'm sure he would have been friends with Joseph. I want so badly to respond to John's death and to Joseph in a way which will keep John's memory alive—will honor his life. I don't wish to give Joseph any more than he has already taken. But oh, it's so difficult, and I miss John so much.

I really had to face the man responsible for my brother's death. I saw him coming and going next door, saw him *living* while my brother was dead. It was a long summer. I felt very alone. Once again I wrote Wilma.

> I wholeheartedly agree with your thoughts of experiencing over and over the whole issue of forgiving the offender. For me this has become even more real and difficult within the last two weeks, as I have discovered that Joseph is my neighbor's stepson and has been living next door to us for the last three weeks. Every day I see his car come and go and see him, too, as he goes about his daily business. I have not yet found the right moment to tell Walt . . . so I am basically left alone to deal with this. It's been difficult, I can assure you.
>
> I have always known that alcohol is used liberally in the home next door. That too makes it difficult. I see Joseph walking on the yard with a case of beer and hear the other neighbors tell me how he comes home late at night, drunk. . . .

I recounted again my discovery of his living next door and my realization of how difficult God's way can be. "But still, that's the way I want to go since I believe that's the only way I can creatively respond to John's death and to the man responsible for it."

Those words looked and sounded good on paper. But the struggle with my anger was still evident.

> I have many mixed feelings about him. I suppose I always will. I still would like to actually hear him verbalize the remorse I suspect (and hope) he feels. But for now I suppose I must accept what he does offer when I see him. By not telling me to leave him alone, he already says something of his feelings. And if he really doesn't feel sorry or guilty, then I suppose I should feel very sorry for him; what kind

of human being could commit an act such as this and not feel anything?

I tell myself repeatedly, too, that I am doing this for my own personal healing and hope that Joseph will wonder why I would choose such a route. Perhaps he will see another way of living. I don't know. I really have no expectations of him and certainly don't expect to change him.

Writing those letters helped. But as Wilma told me in her first letter, this was a personal journey. I could tell myself what I wanted to achieve but couldn't forever suppress my feelings. Feelings are never conjured intentionally. They originate independently and have a life of their own. It's important to name and acknowledge them when they do surface. Otherwise, they begin to control the body they inhabit. Such were my thoughts.

In September I received another letter from Wilma. She suggested I see the movie *Gandhi* and that I think of something I could give Joseph. "The way to overcome evil is, not only forgiveness, but to actually give something of love to that person."

I couldn't answer immediately. I didn't know what to answer. I thought I had already given him a lot. After all, I had told him I didn't wish to hate him. I had "allowed" him to live next door without harassing him. What more could I give? I was stunned, but I kept Wilma's challenge in mind.

In October, as an assignment in a writing class I was taking, I wrote an article on "drinking and driving." What began as an objective piece with statistics and alternate methods of punishment ended as a story entitled "Mr. Clean."

In it, the narrator, a young woman, is cleaning her toilet and simultaneously reminiscing about her brother's death and the man responsible for it. She compares the two men and wonders how her brother might have responded had he been the one alive today. She envisions Joseph falling headfirst into the toilet she is cleaning. She watches him drown, then flushes the toilet.

My feelings had finally erupted. When I finished writing the story, I was shocked. I hadn't realized how deep my anger was. It frightened me, but it was also cleansing. I had named my feelings.

"This reminds me of an Alfred Hitchcock story," my oldest brother said when he read it. In retrospect, I agree. It was brutal, violent, but it was how I felt then. I don't excuse it. Neither do I need to justify my feelings. Along with the anger, there was always the feeling that I wanted to forgive him. I counted on that feeling winning in the end. I prayed for those feelings.

Eventually they came. Eventually, my feelings of compassion and anger resided side by side, their dwelling places the same size.

11
The Trial

In November Joseph went to court once more. Again I attended. It was difficult. A variety of witnesses, policemen, and other experts described the accident in detail. I relived my initial grief and once again hammered down the reality of John's death. Here's what I wrote when I returned home:

> *Today, driving to the preliminary hearing*
> *of my brother's killer, Joseph,*
> *I passed a sign,*
> *SANTA ARRIVES ON SATURDAY.*
>
> *Dear Santa, dear God:*
> *If I promise to be really, really good,*
> *will you let me wake up*
> *from this awful dream right now?*
> *Because, if this is really happening to me,*
> *I don't like it.*
> *It hurts too much.*

And then this:

Just an Ordinary Day in Clearbrook

This morning I got up, gave my two sons their breakfast, made my oldest son's lunch, ate my breakfast, nursed my infant daughter, drove my sons to their respective schools, and dropped my daughter off at a friend's house. Then I went to the local courthouse to attend the preliminary hearing for Joseph, the man responsible for my brother's death.

It is an ordinary day for the citizens of Clearbrook. And here I am, an ordinary law-abiding citizen, a happily married woman, and a mother of three children. And also a victim of a drinking driver, a victim of a senseless, preventable, unjustifiable tragedy. A statistic.

According to Webster's dictionary a statistic is "a single term or datum in a collection of statistics." And statistics are "a branch of mathematics dealing with the collection, analysis, interpretation, and presentation of masses of numerical data." So where do I go from here? How should a "statistic" behave?

In a way, Joseph was lucky. A judge decided where he should go from there—to a higher court where a judge and jury would decide his fate. But I? I had to choose my own future. No one decided for me.

Where did I go? To this book I think. Here I've tried to collect, analyze, and interpret my thoughts, my feelings, and my translation—of John's death, of my grief, and of my response to Joseph.

Now that the municipal court had found enough evidence to charge Joseph on all three counts, I again remembered Wilma's challenge to give something to Joseph.

Christmas came and went. Still I found no answer. And then this, a February 7, 1988 journal entry:

I had an insight during ensemble practice this last week as we sang "To the Hills" and especially as we sang the words,

"In the Lord I've learned to place my trust/ For his judgments they are tender and his mercies just/ For he's proved beyond a doubt to me/ His watchful love and constancy. . . ."

I suddenly saw my brother John's face, then Joseph's. I realized then that if I believed God was merciful and just toward John, I also had to believe (and allow!) that God would offer Joseph the same mercy. Is this what I can give him, God's grace?

I can't describe the suddenness and profundity of that realization. But I knew this was the answer. I felt relieved. And I also realized that the gift I was giving him wasn't my own; rather, I was simply allowing God to give Joseph a gift. My allowing that was a gift, too. But God's gift of grace was much greater; it was extended simultaneously to both John and Joseph.

Time is a generous thing. It brought me Wilma. It brought me her support and encouragement, which healed. Several weeks after my realization during ensemble practice, I watched a TV documentary on drinking and driving. I was moved and found it hard to sleep afterward.

My journal entry for that night shows this:

At 2:00 a.m. I'm thinking about John and the show I just watched. It was very disturbing. The documentary showed two cases—the first, a thirty-five-year-old repeat offender who looked like a real loser. He had driven while impaired and hit a car head-on, killing a young couple. He had been driving with a suspended license. He received two sixteen-year jail terms.

What intrigued me was how upset his mother, brother, and sister were. When the man was found guilty, both he and his family were obviously shaken. But two lives were gone. What would be justice?

The second offender was a young man, eighteen or so, who had only had a few beers but was impaired. He had gone into the wrong lane and hit a car head-on, too. Its occupants were a couple his own age. The parents of both parties were devastated; neither experienced victory here. After the trial, the father of the dead girl was asked how he felt. "I wonder who has lost more," he said.

He was right, of course. Which is worse—a life snuffed out or a life altered forever by a shadow of guilt clouding everything you do? You eat, sleep, and breathe, always thinking, *I have killed two people.*

Six months passed before I could finally write back to Wilma.

Your question about what I could give to Joseph puzzled me in a way. I felt I had already given Joseph something by approaching him twice and telling him directly to his face that I did not wish to hate him; and secondly, by attempting to do the pacifist, "Christian" thing. I've tried to see things from his perspective.

I wasn't angry when you suggested that I give him something; rather, I was puzzled. I thought long and hard about what more I could give him and then finally one day I found the answer: I must allow him to receive an equal portion of God's grace and mercy as I also expect my dead brother to receive. That was hard.

Today I discovered that the trial date has been postponed from April 25th to October 24th! Apparently Joseph's lawyer withdrew from the case, and he had a difficult time finding another one. He was rejected by four lawyers!

So now again, the difficult task of dealing with my anger against a system which allows a person to be free while my brother's life is over. And having to hear from the crown prosecutor that "he's [Joseph] a dummy, a real dummy" does not make things any easier either. So another challenge. . . .

I realize now that there was something else I included in that letter, something of great significance. I told Wilma I'd be open to sharing my story in the newspaper she worked for. That was a sign of healing, I believe, a sign that I could now allow others to share in my pain.

I was looking for ways to creatively and publicly forgive Joseph. In sharing my story I would not only publicize my pain and grief, I would also expose a human Joseph to society. I was, I realize now, giving him more than God's grace. I was trying to be gracious, too. I was even trying to control my anger at the trial's postponement to make room for grace and forgiveness.

Wilma was a safety net for my feelings. In corresponding with me, she gave me a safe and understanding place to air my anger. In encouraging me to submit an article, she enlarged that arena to include (as I discovered after my piece was published) other supportive people.

The title for my article came unbidden. "Who Is My Neighbor?" was the obvious choice. The rest didn't come as quickly.

As I often do, I visited the Benedictine monastery, overlooking the town of Mission. It was a cool, cloudy Sunday afternoon when I drove up the narrow, winding driveway. Dark, heavy clouds hung from the sky, lightly grazing the treetops on the slope leading to the park bench where I usually sit.

Before walking to the bench, I stopped at the chapel. I stood in the entrance, gazing at the stained glass windows on the sides and ceiling of the high, domed interior. I slowly moved to the side and looked at the marble plaques beneath each window. Each plaque showed a scene from Christ's life. The first was a picture of Christ supported by two women, one on each side.

It was like a slap in my face, this picture, for it transported me back to the courthouse where I had first encountered Joseph. Like Christ, he had stood before me, supported by a woman on either side.

The picture unnerved me. I moved away, barely glancing at the other pictures, lest they too become something they were not. As I was about to leave, I noticed a solitary wooden statue. I nearly missed it, for it stood in an unlit corner, in a corridor leading away from the sanctuary. I stood there for a long time, gazing up at that magnificent—but lonely—piece of carved cedar.

Finally, just before I left, I reached up and gently touched the smooth, cold, wooden arm. There was a large, ugly crack on the wrist and another—this one glued—on the upper arm. A small, tattered, cardboard sign hung to the left of the statue. "In memory of St. Joseph, the silent one. May this statue remind us of all the lonely and forgotten."

Again I was unnerved. Was God trying to tell me something? I hurried out of the chapel and to the park bench.

There I waited for my story. It didn't come. My pen and paper didn't meet at all. All I felt was cold from the wind around me. I packed my writing materials, walked back to my van, and headed down the driveway. I wasn't ready to go home—my purpose for coming had been, after all, to write a story.

So I stopped at the cemetery. And there, sitting in my van next to my brother's grave site, it hit me. What I had seen and experienced in the chapel was my story. I began putting my thoughts onto the paper pressed against my steering wheel.

There's blood on my street, thick and red, and it's permanently etched there between my neighbor's driveway and my own. No amount of rain, snow, sun, or even rubber tires will ever erase what this blood spells: *Who Is My Neighbor?*

The words flowed easily now as I recounted my brother's accident, my discovery of Joseph's living next door, my correspondence with Wilma and her challenge.

Today is May, May 1. How appropriate, I think. Mayday! Mayday! My thoughts return to this morning when I was coming out of my house to go to church.

"Hey, Elsie," my neighbor, Mr. Dixon, called to me, just as I was putting on my seatbelt. I rolled down my window.

"Hey, Elsie," he began again, sounding somewhat sheepish. "Do you think you could tell your boys to stay out of my backyard? I mean, they, uh, have been running through my garden."

"Have you?" I turned to them and asked. All the while I was thinking, *A life for a garden, a life for a garden. What's the difference?* Mr. Dixon had never even mentioned my brother's death to me, even though he knew right from the start that it was my brother whom his stepson had killed. He had often had the opportunity to tell me this as we spoke across the fence.

"I didn't, but Matthew did," Daniel confessed from the back seat.

"Did you?" I asked Matthew.

"Yes," he replied.

"Well, then, please say you're sorry to Mr. Dixon." I forced the words out.

"Sorry," said Matthew, somewhat reluctantly.

Sorry? I thought. *Sorry? Oh, God, what next?* Just last week I had finally been able to answer Wilma's question "What can you give to Joseph?" with "I will give him God's grace and forgiveness as I also expect my dead brother to receive."

And now this, another slap on my face. *How many times must I turn my cheek, God?*

Another thought suddenly comes to me, this one as sharp as a knife: Joseph. The statue at the monastery that I just left; its name was Joseph, too. Joseph, my neighbor. Lonely? Forgotten?

My story concluded with Christ's answer to the question of who is my neighbor? Jesus answered with the story of the good Samaritan, followed by the question: "Which of these . . . . was a neighbor?"

Other questions arose for me. What should I do? And what should I say to Joseph, to Mr. Dixon, both of whom had never even said to me, "I'm sorry."

I thought my experience at the cemetery might conclude my struggle. It didn't. The questions persisted.

But I wasn't discouraged. In writing and submitting that article I was at least on the right path. That was what counted, that I was going in the right direction.

Once again I realized how desperately I still wished for an apology. For a while that became my focus. Why couldn't he, or at least his family (who continued to live next door to me), apologize? Two words were all I wanted: "I'm sorry." I would have said it if I were them. Why couldn't they do that for me?

As before, writing stories became the vehicle for dealing with this ongoing struggle. I think that when you desire something deeply, all life is seen through that request. I wanted to hear an apology. I interpreted events around me through that desire.

One night in June, while driving home after dropping off our babysitter, I had an accident. The road I drove on was familiar; as I approached the hill I slowed down. To my left I could see a large dog running toward my van. I braked hard, but there was nothing I could do. The dog and van met. Shocked, I continued driving. I could hear the dog yelping behind me, could see in my rearview mirror the wet trail he left behind, as he dragged himself to the side of the road.

I couldn't keep going. I turned around to face what I had done. I was shaking as I approached the people surrounding the injured animal.

"There she is," said a young girl with a tear-stained face. She pointed at me.

"Is he all right?" I asked. "I tried to stop, but he ran right into me. There was nothing I could do. I'm so sorry." I began to cry.

"Hey, it's not your fault. It's okay. Really. We saw it happen."

"You don't understand," I said. "My brother was killed a year ago. I'm so sorry." I thrust a paper with my name and phone number at them, then said I had to go.

"Somebody's dog, somebody's brother," I wrote later. "Sorry, sorry. Who will say sorry to me?"

The dog's owner called the next day. The dog wasn't injured badly. I offered again to help pay the veterinarian's bill.

She refused. "It's not your fault," she said. "Take care of yourself, okay?"

"Okay."

Okay? Okay? How can I be okay? I almost killed somebody's dog and I can hardly live with that. What would I do if I hit a person?

Recently someone told me my responses aren't typical. I find that hard to believe. All I try to do is put myself in the other person's shoes. For example, late one evening I heard a vehicle screeching to a halt in front of our house. The sound of loud voices prompted me to go outside to see if someone was in danger. I watched as a young girl jumped out of the vehicle and started walking away. A man then leaped out of the truck and followed her. They were yelling at each other.

"Do you need help?" I shouted to the girl. Even when she declined, I offered again, three more times. Is that unusual? What if I had been in trouble on some dark side street. Wouldn't I want help?

To me, it seems so clear. If you hurt someone, apologize. If you take a life, admit your guilt. I was surprised by the dog owner's response. I expected her to let me help pay the medical costs, even though it wasn't my fault. I expected her to be angry, but she wasn't. She was gracious and kind. I would want to be, too.

Perhaps that's why Joseph has never apologized. Perhaps he's afraid of me. Or perhaps he's afraid of himself, of his feelings about what he has done. Perhaps an apology to me would make him drown in the reality of what he did that night. Maybe he can't even forgive himself.

The dog incident shook me up. Not only because it recalled my feelings about John's death, but, I think, because I experienced an accident. I have never had a speeding ticket or been in an automobile accident. Hitting that dog showed me how quickly it can happen—even when you're paying attention, even when you try to prevent it. I felt helpless. I saw the dog, I braked, I heard the impact, I felt the pain. Was that how Joseph felt?

Another summer passed. This one was so unlike the last, when I had often sat in our backyard, looking at the next-door neighbors. At times, I felt the feelings of unfairness surface again. This was the second summer my brother had been denied, yet Joseph was free. Still, the times of focusing on the man responsible for John's death were coming less often. That felt hopeful.

It was a summer of beauty. We traveled through the Rockies to southern Alberta, where the canola-yellowed hills were like gentle waves after a storm. Another week spent on Saltspring Island was like a gift from heaven. Never had the ocean looked so beautiful; never had a starry summer night looked down on me with such tenderness and love; never had the sound of waves crashing on the rocks calmed and soothed my soul like now. God's signature was all over these sights. Would I have seen God's words of love and comfort written there had I not struggled so with facing my enemy? I doubt it.

12
Forgiving
and Freeing

Autumn came. The trees sang to me and I recorded their song in this poem.

AUTUMNAL GRACE AND HOPE

Fall is here!
Colors splash on browning grass below,
gently ricochet, then softly land
and lie there, motionless.
Bits of disconnected trees
now feed the earth.
Yellow, orange, and flaming red,
at first a blanket for the dying grass,
they slowly wilt, then rot.
Scattered pieces wash away,
entwine with blades of grass and weeds
and other things decayed,
till all that's left is bare, brown soil,
now richer.

Earth, receive with open arms the rains
the falling sky bestows on you.
For pain and death give birth
to wealth not dreamed of.
Receive with joy the gifts
that follow sin and guilt.
Christ has come! The fallen leaf
at last redeemed.
Forgiveness hangs from every branch
stripped bare by autumn.

With the whisper of those words, autumn offered me forgiveness. And I responded; I reached up and picked the fruit of grace. Several weeks later, Joseph had his final days in court.

What a strange thing, to attend the trial of a man responsible for the death of my brother, a man the same age as my brother.

In a sense, attending the trial was another death. The death of my innocence. John's death had shattered my life. But it had had little impact on the rest of society.

The bailiff, the court stenographer, and all the other court attendants carried on. Sitting in that courtroom, biding their time from one paycheck to the next. What did it matter to them that John was dead? Their slouched postures and yawns told me everything I needed to know.

"Hey, my brother is dead!" I wanted to shout.

Instead, I watched the jurors enter, watched the crown counsel and defending lawyer enter, then watched *him* enter. I watched him sit on the blood-colored leather chair, enclosed at sides and back with glass walls. For protection?

"What does he look like?" my mother often asked.

"Mom, I could be describing John," I always answered.

Again today I saw the similarities. Dark, thick hair, thick moustache, nice-looking face, though his brown eyes certainly don't contain the life John's did. His casual but neat apparel—yellow sweater, brown corduroy pants— could have been John's. But he wasn't John.

Joseph's sisters, the ones who were with him at the initial court appearance, sat behind my sister Margaret and me. Their heads met as often as ours. How were they feeling? Such parallels. Two sets of sisters, a few feet apart—each there because of a thirty-two-year-old brother.

Would I want to exchange places with them? No! Nor would I want John alive and in that chair, the reason for this trial. But it could have been. What would I have whispered to my sister then? What would I have hoped to hear the jury saying then? And if John were sitting in that chair, what would his face be like? Would it have been as lifeless as Joseph's was today?

I think he would have cried, cried a lot. So maybe, just maybe, I should cry for Joseph now. Perhaps if he can't cry about what he's done, then I and all of us who knew and loved John should cry for Joseph.

The trial ended on the third day, at high noon. At 6:00 p.m. the jury came back. Guilty. On all three charges. Sentencing was set for three weeks later.

"How do you feel?" I was asked.

"Like there are no winners; we are all losers."

The only relief I felt was that the formalities of this part of John's death would soon be over.

What did I want the trial to accomplish? Above all, I wanted it to affirm the value of a life, of John's life. Are three days enough? No! But at least during three days John's death affected other lives.

Life can't just go on and be the same when someone dies. It has to make a difference. If it doesn't, what is life worth? Why was John alive? Why should I go on living? If in the end it makes no difference, why continue? That trial at least affirmed that John had made some impact.

The guilty verdict also was important to me. Not for revenge, but because it assigned responsibility. It said *someone* caused John's death. Again, it comes down to the value of a life. Someone needs to take responsibility for such a death. It never "just happens" just as life is never "just lived."

On November 4, 1988, two weeks before the sentencing, I went to a friend's place to use the computer. I wrote a letter to the judge on behalf of my sister and me.

"What is justice? Our family has often asked this since the death of our brother, John Victor Klassen, on March 15th of last year," I wrote. Then I answered.

There is, of course, no sufficient answer, only another question; of what value is a life? Is it three days in court? Is it a lifetime of having one's driver's license revoked? Is it a year or two, or ten or twenty, or even a lifetime spent in prison? Is is worth a death sentence?

The answer to all of these questions is, of course, "no." A life is worth much more; a life of value always deserves another chance.

For our brother John it is too late. He is dead. It is impossible for him to have another chance at life. Likewise, it is also impossible for us to have another chance to touch him, talk to him, hold him, or tell him we love him.

John's death has already brought enough devastation into our own family. For that reason, we now seek to honor his life by suggesting a creative punishment for the person responsible for John's death. This is not to say that we want to minimize the horror and devastation of this offense. Rather, we wish to recognize that Joseph's life is also a life of value. He, too, has a family who laments his ruined life.

In declaring Joseph guilty of causing John's death, the court has assigned him the awesome task of assuming the responsibility for taking another person's life, the life of a man his own age. A life of someone's son and brother, a life of someone's friend and uncle. Which of us would wish to carry such a burden? And what type of punishment could surpass that? Wouldn't it be better to ask what we could do to prevent this from happening again? We think so.

And so we come to this court with several requests, realizing that in doing so take a great risk. We ask:

(1) that if Mr. Dixon receive a prison sentence, it be served in a minimum security prison;

(2) that Mr. Dixon's driver's license be suspended for an appropriate amount of time. A driver's license is a privilege, not a right. Mr. Dixon has abused that privilege and it now must be withdrawn.

(3) that Mr. Dixon be required to work with an anti-drunk driving organization to help create public awareness of the potentially tragic results of irresponsible drinking;

(4) that Mr. Dixon be required to do some sort of community work in order to repay some of the costs that this crime has incurred.

It is our sincere desire that reconciliation occur, both between Joseph and our family, and the community and Joseph. If it would help him or his family to meet with members of our family, we would be willing to meet.

Perhaps these suggestions could be a beginning to alternative methods of preventative punishments for such horrendous, but avoidable, crimes.

November 20, 1988

The drive into the New Westminster courthouse was a long one. I wondered what it must feel like to be in Joseph's shoes. How would it feel to know that by this afternoon you might be in a prison cell?

The sentencing room was small; there were only two benches for spectators. We sat behind Joseph's family, whose members occupied the whole row in front of us. They were as nervous as we. They had more to lose than we. Our brother's fate had already been sealed.

The minutes dragged as we sat and waited for the defendant. "He's out looking for his lawyer," I heard the crown counsel whisper. My sister and I didn't need to verbalize our thoughts—we wouldn't want him as our lawyer.

Another half hour. They appeared. "All rise," and "order in the court." Surely I was watching someone else's story.

I listened to the crown counsel's final speech, heard the defendant's lawyer rearrange my careful words. Had he any idea how much they cost, these words he tossed around so casually?

"Even the family is asking for leniency," he said.

I shifted in my seat, wondering if this was a mistake.

The judge was on my side. He heard my words, my intent. He publicly announced his respect for our requests. Someone heard. Someone cared.

The sentence followed: fifteen months imprisonment in a minimum security prison, two year's license suspension, one hundred hours of community work, one year's probation.

To the sound of his sisters' crying, Joseph was escorted from the room. He turned and weakly smiled at them. It was the first time I saw emotion on his face.

I was torn. Should I lean forward and comfort the weeping ones in front? When they said "It could have been worse," should I have said, "Yes, it could have been and, for us, it was"? I did neither. I just sat there watching, thinking, *Now it's finally over.*

■ ■ ■

I am a doorperson, I thought later that day as I wandered restlessly through the rooms of my house. A doorperson. Have you ever noticed doorpeople? I haven't, at least not often.

Doorpeople have important tasks. They don't simply open and close doors. They're the face of the establishment for which they open doors. They make the first impression on visitors.

Doorpeople, even though they wear uniforms, don't have high profiles, especially if they do their tasks well. With one smooth motion their arms open the doors. They're often so subtle that the person walking through doesn't even notice them.

When the weather is stormy, the doorperson is most often noticed. Strange, because then people are in a big hurry to get into warm, dry shelter. But it's also in these times that the opened door is most appreciated.

Hands and doors seem to go together. I recall the picture of Jesus knocking at the door, waiting to be let in. That door never opened. I always wished it would. As a child, I got tired of looking at Jesus standing there, forever knocking, knocking.

The doors in Egypt were bloodstained, painted with the blood of slaughtered lambs, a symbol that God wanted Pharaoh to let God's people go. *Open the door, Pharaoh, and let my people out!* How long did those bloodstains stay on those doors? How long afterward did the Egyptians suffer for not opening those doors?

On the afternoon of Halloween, I took my sons over to my neighbors. Together we would be doorpeople and help Mr. Dixon walk into the room called forgiveness.

"Mom, I really don't want to do this," Daniel repeatedly told me. Matthew kept saying, "What did you say we should tell him? I keep forgetting."

"Tell him you're sorry for cutting the branches off his tree, and tell him you won't do it again," I said, for the tenth time.

The boys slowly shuffled up the steps and rang the doorbell. "No one home," Daniel said, turning away.

"Try again," I said. "There's a light on inside."

Matthew knocked and rang the doorbell.

The door opened. "Hi, boys," Mr. Dixon said.

"We're sorry we cut the branches from your tree and promise not to do it again," Daniel said, all in one breath.

"Well," said Mr. Dixon, "I'll forgive you on one condition. Stay off my lawn and don't saw on my trees again, okay?" He smiled.

"Okay," they both said.

The door closed and we returned home.

"He was nice, wasn't he, Mom? He didn't even get mad," said Daniel.

"Yes, he was nice," I said.

This was the second time in the past six months I had asked the boys to apologize to Mr. Dixon for invading his property. Twice I had knocked at his door. When would I open my front door to find him standing there, apologizing for the death his stepson had caused?

How long was the bloodstain on the door of the Israelites? Longer than the black mark on the side of the road where my brother's car exploded? It is still there.

The day after the sentencing I woke with laryngitis. I lay on the couch, whispering to my daughter, as she romped around the room. The phone rang.

"Hello? This is Beulah, your neighbor."

"Oh, hi," I whispered, then explained about my voice.

"Oh," she said. "Well, I won't keep you. I just called to tell you thank you for the nice letter you wrote to the judge. Gee, I'm going to cry. I'm still sick, you know. I just had open-heart surgery. I'm sorry I never talked to you before about this. It's just that it was so horrible.

"Anyway, Tannis [Joseph's sister] asked if she could have copy of the letter. I'll let you go now. You're not feeling well. We'll have to get together for coffee when you get better. Okay?"

"Okay," I said. "Thanks for calling. I appreciate it."

Several hours later Mr. Dixon phoned, not realizing his wife had already called. "I just called to thank you for writing the letter," he said very slowly. "I haven't read it but I sure have heard a lot about it."

"Thank you," I squeaked out.

"Boy, you sure sound sick," he said. "What's wrong?"

"Laryngitis," I replied, then asked how he was feeling. He has cancer.

"Well, we all have to suffer," he said. "You don't know what enjoyment is until you've suffered. This has been terrible for all of us. I'm just glad Joseph didn't have to go to a maximum security prison with all those criminals. He's a nice guy; he doesn't belong there."

"No, he doesn't," I said.

"Well, you take care of yourself," he said.

I cried.

It's hard being a doorperson. People take you for granted. They think you're just doing a menial job. They think you're not qualified to do anything else. What they don't understand is how crucial the timing is. Open the door too quickly and people might not come in. They weren't planning to use that door; you just assumed they were. Open the door too slowly and they might change their minds and go elsewhere. Yes, timing is crucial.

On Christmas Eve I went over to my neighbors. I had a card, and had photocopied the letter they had requested. No one was home. I left the card in the screen door, hoping they would see it before the wind blew it away.

The next day, as I was coming into the living room, a hand reached through the mail slot. A card dropped to the floor. Then the hand was gone. It hadn't knocked, just dropped these words in: "Dear Walter, Elsie, and boys: All the best to you. Merry Christmas. Sincerely, Cast and Beulah." Another step through the door.

I'll always feel remnants of anger. But I've reached my goal—grace has won the race. Only occasionally do the other feelings again threaten to take the lead. February 27, John's birthday, is a hard day. Christmas, when our family gathers, screams out the absence of a brother, son, and uncle. Easter, as we relive Christ's death, is painful too, but promises we shall meet again someday.

There are evenings when Walt is working and the children are asleep. Sometimes I think I hear a knock at the door, and, for a moment I pretend it's John. But it's only the wind. Or is it?

Have I forgiven? I think so. I do each day. Last week my daughter fell and cut her nose. Instinctively, I told my son, "Run get the neighbor. Tell him I need help."

Two minutes later Cast arrived, genuine concern on his face. "What's wrong, Elsie?"

When I explained that I couldn't drive and hold Rachel, he ran home and returned with his truck.

The drive to the hospital was awkward. Cast kept assuring me, "It'll be all right."

As we neared the hospital, I realized I had instinctively trusted him. Even more important, I had provided him with a door to redemption, and he had walked through.

I've learned a lot through this experience. The way of God, of forgiveness, is hard but worth following. I'm not a saint. Therefore I appreciate the model of Christ. Prior to this experience, I assumed Christ's responses came easily and naturally. Now I believe otherwise. Christ, in assuming humanity, surely must have experienced the same feelings and difficulties as I did through this encounter. Because of that, he understands my struggles.

Christ never promised an easy road, but he promised that "the truth will set you free." I've claimed that promise, I've trusted that promise, and now I've experienced that promise. Each time I look into my neighbor's yard, I'm being freed. So are they. I'm thankful.

Where Was God?

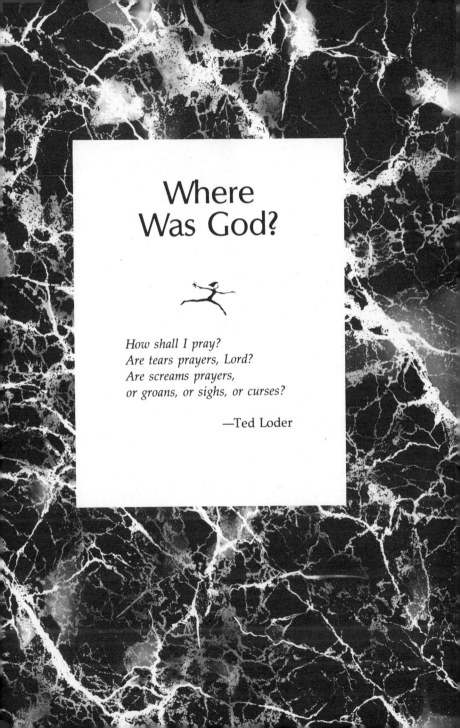

How shall I pray?
Are tears prayers, Lord?
Are screams prayers,
or groans, or sighs, or curses?

—Ted Loder

13
God with Us!

This book wouldn't be complete without asking, *Where was God when John was killed?*

I'm not a trained theologian. I've gleaned my biblical knowledge primarily from my church, the Christian high school I attended, a fundamentalist Bible school I attended for a year (whose theology I have left behind), and my own personal studies. But I still feel a need to share my thoughts about God's role in all of this.

For me, it's almost blasphemous to suggest God would cause an event like John's death. Shortly after John died, I wrote a letter to friends in which I said, "If my theology had not changed as it did in the last three years, my faith wouldn't have sustained me through John's death."

It's true. I'm a thinking, introspective person who doesn't easily accept quick answers, plastic solutions. Some of my theological thoughts may offend some; they may point to my lack of theological expertise.

I'll take that risk. Not to prove a point, but hoping that my thoughts will help others who wish to strengthen their faith in God through such events as these.

When someone dies, the person left behind usually takes a new look at God. Sometimes the death diminishes God, and God becomes microscopic. "What kind of God would allow this to happen?" is the question which shrinks this once all-powerful God.

Some people cower under the power of a God who looks down on humanity and randomly chooses to inflict suffering. The God they once trusted to be loving and kind has suddenly become an omnipotent tyrant.

Others conclude there is no God. Not only does God disappear, often the person's own meaning and reason for existence disappear as well. Why are we here? And how did we get here? These are the questions which become the focus. Is there any direction or purpose for life's events?

Matthew came home from school one day distraught. "I hate Santa Claus," he said. "In fact, I think there might not even be such a thing as Santa Claus."

"Oh?" I said, wondering about the origin of this pronouncement.

"Well, Christmas has come and gone, and he still hasn't brought me the things I asked for. He's bad, Santa is bad." His face was a sullen mask.

"Well," I suggested carefully, "did he actually promise to bring *all* the things you asked for?"

"Well, no."

"Then why are you so disappointed in him? He didn't promise anything; he only listened to your requests. You're the one who expected him to obey your orders, right?"

"Well, yes. But I still don't think he's real."

I think many people are like Matthew. They expect God to be who they want God to be, not the I AM WHO I AM of the Bible. People decide for themselves, at their own convenience, which events resurrect or kill God.

I feel fortunate that I had already asked a lot of "why" questions prior to John's death. I had come to understand that some questions can never fully be answered. Maybe finding answers is less important than asking the right questions. Questions which lead to growth and peace are preferable to the questions leading faith to dead-end roads. This understanding helped me immensely after John died.

For me, John's death put a magnifying glass on God. My God suddenly expanded—but paradoxically, he was also near and intimate enough to cradle me in divine hands. Not bound by time or space like humans, God can see the whole of life, from start to finish.

When John first died, I felt I needed to "save" him, so I could rest assured he had gone to heaven. My quest to redeem John was matched by my quest to explain that God hadn't willed John's gruesome death. I felt I needed to excuse God either way, whether God caused it or didn't prevent it.

But I came to see I needn't do either. God is who God is. And John was who he was. My task isn't to define or explain either. My primary task as a Christian is to live life to the fullest, in a style imitative of Christ.

Luci Shaw, an American poet, wrote a wonderful book called *A Widening Light: Poems of the Incarnation*. In it she includes a poem titled "Judas, Peter." As does Christ when he tells the self-righteous Pharisees not to cast stones at the prostitute unless they were without sin, Shaw reminds me to focus on my own life rather than judging others lives.

> *because we are all*
> *betrayers, taking*
> *silver and eating*
> *body and blood and asking*

(guilty) is it I and hearing
him say yes
it would be simple for us all
to rush out and hang ourselves
but if we find grace
to cry and wait
after the voice of morning
has crowed in our ears
clearly enough
to break our hearts
he will be there
to ask us each again
do you love me?

And so I directed my energy away from all those difficult and humanly unanswerable questions. I tried instead to focus on the call of Christ: "Do you love me?" The process has stretched my understanding of God.

Also critical to my change in focus were these words: "Some people would rather send a person to hell than believe in the grace of God." Powerful words, this woman's, but not spoken lightly. Her son had committed suicide.

She was right. We consign to hell so casually, so thoughtlessly. Yet how often do we ask for grace to cover our own countless sins? Don't we believe God grants us grace even when we repeat our mistakes? Did God withhold grace from the man who hung beside God's son, after that man simply recognized who Christ was?

I can't prove these thoughts. I no longer think I must. I simply want to respond to the call of God to listen, look, and learn, and, by my living, to answer the question, "Do you love me?" I want to learn more of God even in the midst of all this pain. In doing so, I've experienced the often inexpressible miracle of healing and peace. What paradox: I feel pain in order to heal; God is vast, but God is near.

God is grace incarnate. And I am a being created in the image of a God whose most powerful tool to bring humanity into redeemed, restored relationship is divine grace. Now, humbly aware of my humanity and sin, I must model God's grace for others. When I do this, when I attempt to love and forgive others, it is only because God loved and forgave me first. How true the words of 2 Corinthians 12:9-10, NIV:

> [9]But he said to me, "My grace is sufficient for you, for my power is made perfect in weakness." Therefore I will boast all the more gladly about my weaknesses, so that Christ's power may rest on me. [10]That is why, for Christ's sake, I delight in weaknesses, in insults, in hardships, in persecutions, in difficulties. For when I am weak, then I am strong.

Yes, my role and focus have changed, from being heaven's realtor to being a servant of God and a grace-giver. That's how I try to live now. I try to energize and enable others by offering grace to them. I don't mean to advocate universal salvation or condone sin. But sin is and always will be part of our human condition, Christian or not. If we judge others only on the basis of their sin, will not God so judge us? I believe strongly that God is more gracious than we can understand. And when it comes to our eternal destination, God will judge justly, according to divine, not human, law.

But where was this almighty and gracious God when John was killed? When I went to be with my parents on the morning of John's death, my father said, "We always prayed for John, every night. Why didn't God hear? Why wasn't God there?"

"God was there," I said immediately, instinctively. "If

you asked God to be with John, then God was there."

Do I really believe this? Yes, yes! God was there; my father requested it. But did God cause the accident? No! God was there, watching, anguished, weeping at the fate of one of God's own created beings. God was wracked with pain, as only a parent can be when witnessing the death of a child by the hand of another.

I also believe this: it didn't end there. God didn't vacate the earth after that horrible sight. I think God held John's hand in death.

I think of a picture which used to hang in my grandmother's house; when Grandma died, John chose to have that picture. It wasn't great art. The frame was made of mirrored glass, and over the years the picture beneath the glass faded and wrinkled. But that picture left an impression on me—and obviously on John. He hung it in the last house he lived in—the same house Grandma once lived in.

The picture was of two small children, a boy and a girl, crossing a bridge suspended above a raging river. The children, who both looked terrified, held hands. Above them hovered an angel, its arms held open, an umbrella of protection.

God's hand was there. I choose to believe that. It is a promise God makes repeatedly in the Bible, in all the stories of God's interaction with God's human offspring. To focus on the promise that God is with us in such tragedies is to choose hope and life in an otherwise hopeless situation.

Consider God's promises in Isaiah 42:5-6 and 43:1-2, NIV:

> [5]This is what God the Lord says—
> he who created the heavens and stretched them out,
> who spread out the earth and all that comes out of it,
> who gives breath to its people,

and life to those who walk on it:
⁶"I, the Lord, have called you in righteousness;
I will take hold of your hand."

"Fear not, for I have redeemed you;
I have called you by name; you are mine.
²When you pass through the waters,
I will be with you;
and when you pass through the rivers,
they will not sweep over you.
when you walk through the fire,
you will not be burned;
the flames will not set you ablaze.
³For I am the Lord your God,
the Holy One of Israel, your Savior.

There is more. God's hand lay on our family, too, working through the many people who came to mourn with us. Each hug and handshake we received was human, yes, but had its roots in the love of God.

In her book, *What Was Good About Today?*, Carol Kruckeberg, learned her nine-year-old Sara has leukemia. She asked her minister,

> "Where is it, Elmer? Father, Son and Holy Ghost. Our Father, who art in heaven. Sara believes. Well, why haven't we heard from Good Old God, Elmer? Why?"
>
> Elmer didn't answer immediately, just shrugged and pulled at his beard. His answer was another question. "What does hold you together?" he asked.
>
> "The phone calls. The letters. Our family. Our friends. They shoulder in close. And sometimes they lift us above it all. That's what," she answered.
>
> Elmer's response to that? "Maybe there's your big booming voice. Worth considering anyway."

I agree. I too believe God visits and comforts us most tangibly through others. A man from my parent's church stopped by to see my parents after John died. Before he left, he put his hand on my father's arm and said, with tear-filled eyes, "If I could take this from you, I would."

If I could take this from you, I would. I believe that God, if God spoke in human words, would say the same. What more is there to say than *if I could*?

But God could have and didn't. Could God, really, without removing other things as well? And would we really want God to if it meant giving up those things?

Several years ago, friends of ours had an encephalitic baby. One month before Katie was to give birth, the doctor told her that the baby would be born dead. After a long labor she gave birth. The boy's body and face were perfect. His brain wasn't. He lived three days. During that entire time, she kept him with her and held him.

Several months later, I asked whether she would have terminated the pregnancy if she had known the outcome.

"No," she immediately answered. She'd do it over again, she said, just the way it had happened. She had been told the child would be born dead but she had held him for three days. Those three days had cushioned the pain which followed her son's death.

If my family had been given a choice between having John with us for thirty-two years, or not having him at all, we all would have chosen to have him. John's life was worth the pain his death has brought. His life magnified both God and all life. Life is much more precious than it was before, for I am trying now to live with the assumption that it could end at any moment.

And finally, if my understanding of the God of the Bible, especially as described in the books of Genesis and 1 John, is correct, then this God I worship is the author of *life*, not death. That is my mandate also, to create life—and through that to answer God's question to me, "Do you love me?"

14

Hope in God

I visited a local Christian bookstore and came across several books about children and death. Out of curiosity, I picked one up and paged through. I was shocked.

I read about a woman who gave birth to a handicapped child who died several months later. That in itself wasn't appalling. What disturbed me was her attributing the birth, the handicap, and the subsequent death to God's will—God wanted to teach her a lesson.

I asked myself how a loving God could prescribe this nightmare? Why would a loving God decide a particular woman needs to be taught a lesson through the death of her handicapped baby? For me the answer is clear: a loving God would *not* do such a thing. Such death would hurt God as much as the parent herself.

I think of the events surrounding Christ's death. The Bible tells us that darkness descended on the earth, the curtain in the temple ripped open, and an earthquake shook the land. Some interpret these events as symbols of a new era, an age when the temple and sacrifices were no longer required.

I think something deeper happened. I believe the events surrounding Christ's death were God's audible grief, translated into a language we could see and hear.

Who can deny the power of an electrical storm or an earthquake? God *screamed* when Christ died. God didn't want Christ to die, *but there was no other way*. Christ prayed for another way: "My Father, if it is possible, may this cup to be taken from me. Yet not as I will, but as you will" (Matthew 26:42, NIV). Isn't that a prayer spoken for all who mourn today? And isn't God's response then also God's response now? God doesn't want people to die. But there is no other way! Christ died at humanity's hand (the people chose!) and now too, people die at the hands of others.

So often people ask, "Why would God do this?" and expect an answer. The emphasis is on the *why*. I'd like to ask the same question with a different emphasis. Why *would* God do this? I don't believe God would.

Earlier I said that death, for some people, diminishes God. I think such an attitude also diminishes people. For if God deliberately planned such things and randomly executed these plans in the lives of people, then aren't we puppets, pawns in the game of life?

What kind of God would whisper in my brother's ear on a particular evening, telling him to travel down a certain road so another car would kill him? Would any person plot such a thing for a friend, a brother, a child? Would a Creator do such a thing to the creation?

I believe God screamed when John died. Loudly. No, not in thunder or in earthquakes, but through me, through the voice I woke to in the days following John's death. And in the voices of all who cried then and still cry for John. Isn't it logical that a God who comforts us through people would also *cry* through us?

Elie Wiesel, survivor of the Holocaust and a storyteller, once said God loves stories; that's why God created people. If it's true that all our lives are stories, why would God, the author, cut some stories short before their ending? Would a writer do this? Why publish a half-written or barely begun story? Unless, of course, the author meant to irritate or tease the readers.

No, I don't think God would do such a thing, just as I wouldn't dangle an unfinished story before my readers. God is loving, just, and above all a life-giver. God wants us to live as much as we wish to live. God doesn't want us to suffer. God does not want illness, war, or accidents to cut short our lives.

I do believe God has the power to prevent death and could have prevented John's death. But I wouldn't want God to exercise that power if that made me God's puppet. I want to live as God's creation, exercising creativity as my Creator did and does. I also want to worship God at my initiative, not in response to a command but in self-chosen love and gratitude for God's gift of freedom.

If indeed God wills such things, I lose the freedom to choose my response. Then the only response I can offer is silence. I shouldn't question, shouldn't feel anything about John's death. I should bow my head in resignation to John's death and everything else around me.

Then I can only say one thing: "It was God's will." But then who next? Who will God take to teach my next lesson? My husband, my children, my friends?

That's not my God. I could never be silent. And if I should be required to be silent and fearful at the same time, I wouldn't wish further relationship with a God who demanded only silence and fear.

My Creator God is big. John's death *has* magnified this God a hundredfold. And I have responded creatively, I think. This book is my creative response, my act of gratitude to God for enabling me to walk through and grow from this experience. And I believe it was God who gave me the talent to respond in my own way.

John's life was a story. But it wasn't over. My life's a story, too. But my story won't be what it might have been had John not died, for we define each others' stories. Now my challenge is to live my story without John. My story needs reworking. God gives me strength to do so. I live my story feeling blessed that I, because God gave me choice, can choose my own response.

Death, as I said earlier, murders feelings, but God's redemptive love resurrects them, if we let it. If we choose to cling only to the "why" questions, which often lead to hate, bitterness, and endless frustration, we won't find new life. But trusting is to choose life, not death.

Forgiveness, especially in my case, can't change the past, but it can open a door to the future. Bitterness never opens doors; it only closes them. "Why" couldn't have brought me to this place, nor can string-pulled puppets climb to lofty places.

I think God celebrates with us when we find meaning after death. The God who walks through light and darkness with us is the God I love. I find true comfort, love, and justice in this God.

For me, the strongest evidence of a God who celebrates with us is the biblical account of events following the crucifixion. Initially, God screamed through earthquakes and thunder. Then God stayed and comforted those who wept at Christ's passing.

I try to imagine how it must have felt to be part of the group visiting Christ's grave. Perhaps it was early morning; mist hung over the place where Christ had been laid to rest. On the horizon, morning reached out and sprinkled flecks of gold on the half-dark sky. Birds sang, their song welcoming the light. The group huddled together, oblivious to the unfolding beauty. Then the sun thrust itself into the day, its long, warm arms reaching out to the crowd below, warming their cool skins. "He is not here," the shout went up. "He is not here."

Last week a woman joining my congregation shared her story. "I'm a person who always asks 'why'," she told us. "Why, after years of fighting going into the ministry, then training for it and being in it for only six months, did my husband have to die, leaving me, at thirty-six, a widow with three children?

"Why, after I married a widower, did my stepdaughter die? Why? Why is my stepson dying now of the same disease that took his mother and sister?"

As she stood before us, sharing her story, I felt hopeless. Like Job, she had earned the right to ask why. It showed her humanness. I listened, spellbound as she unraveled her story. How did she ever find an answer?

With remarkable composure and strength, she told her secret. "Where there is pain, beauty is sure to follow. When I cannot find the beauty, I wait. And I believe, for my life has taught me that it will *always* come, if not in the event itself, then in another event. And so I wait. And I have never been disappointed yet."

I felt ecstatic. "You are the beauty in my day," I told her. "Your story *is* beauty." It was March 15, two years to the day.

Does God cause pain? No. But God is with us in the pain, and God provides beauty to make the pain tolerable. "There is always a counterbalance to pain and suffering; it is beauty." I shall never forget the words I heard that night.

It is so true that "in all things God works for the good of those who love him" (Romans 8:28). But the good is not in the tragic event itself. I look for it elsewhere. It is in God and God's creation, not in death.

New
Pathways

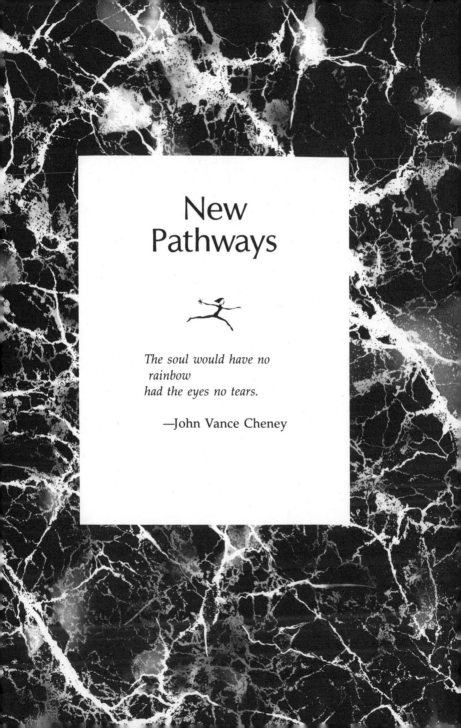

*The soul would have no
  rainbow
had the eyes no tears.*

—John Vance Cheney

15

Grief Recovery

When I was a teenager, my friends and I often participated in car rallies. A car rally is a game in which players follow instructions which lead them to places where they gather clues to answer questions. It's always tempting to speed from one location to the next to finish first. But the rules specifically state that accuracy, not speed, determines the winner. It is more important to locate and stop at each checkpoint within the legal speed limit than to arrive at the finish line first. In fact, often the winner doesn't finish first. The winner is the one who follows the map, takes no shortcuts, deliberately goes through (not around) each instruction *sequentially*.

Larry Yeagley, a hospital chaplain and author of *Grief Recovery*, says:

> When a person goes through grief, he or she is caught between the need to suffer pain and the urge to run.
> The sooner and the more intensely the person experiences suffering, the sooner he recovers. . . . a grieving person should be encouraged to reach out to others and to lean on friends and professional helpers.

Ultimately, a person must go through the pain . . . to be healed . . . .

I think that Grief Recovery and car rallies are a lot alike. After John died, I craved healing. I thought if I pushed myself through the steps I read about in books on mourning, I'd heal quickly. John died in March. I hoped for complete healing by the end of summer. I was disappointed. Not only wasn't my healing complete, I felt completely disassociated from myself.

In retrospect, the first year after John's death was hell. Just when I thought I was getting better, I'd have a setback. Now I can recall little of that endless blur of year. My oldest son went into grade one. I remember little of that. I only remember rising in the morning and going to bed at night. Long, long days and dream-filled nights. Laughter almost always forced; tears easily summoned.

What changed? Many things. But one event stands out. A year after John's death, Betty McMichael, a former neighbor and good friend of John's, called. "Have you heard of 'Grief Recovery'?" she asked, then said she was joining it.

I had seen an ad in the local paper a few weeks earlier and felt interested. But I wasn't sure I felt brave enough to face a circle of strangers with my grief. Now I recognized how much I needed an arena in which to air my grief. I really hadn't talked as much about my grief as I imagined.

The March group, unfortunately, was filled. The next opening would be in September. "Can you wait till then?" Marie Riediger, the facilitator of the group, asked.

"Yes," I said, "I think I can."

Meanwhile, the first group completed the course and began meeting as a support group. When Betty called to invite me to that monthly meeting, I accepted. Sixteen months had passed since John's death. Now, on this neutral ground, Betty and I met for the first time since the funeral. We embraced, and in that moment John's death became reality. It had been an overdue meeting for both of us, but for some reason had been too difficult.

In September I joined fourteen others and committed myself to five sessions of Grief Recovery.

"What makes grieving so difficult?" was the question which launched our meetings. It was an invitation to open all our locked-up grief. Only we could provide the keys. "You must go *through* the pain, *not* around it," we were told, "and then you will find healing."

It was a grueling session, and as forewarned, I left with the question, "Why am I doing this?"

But that's not all I left with. I left with status. I was now recognized. I finally had "mourner" status. Siblings had a right to mourn like any other group. And I was given instructions, a recipe for normal, healthy grieving.

Grief Recovery was a rally for my emotions. The first hand-out we received was entitled, "Journey of Grief." On it was a picture of a valley. On the left, beneath a cloud-filled sky, was the descent. On the right, beneath a sunny sky, was the ascent. Markers along the way gave direction: *loss, protest, searching, despair, reorganization, reinvestment*. Interestingly, there were no speed limits. But neither were there short cuts.

"How deeply you grieve and how long you grieve depends on the type of loss you have experienced. No two people grieve the same way," our instructor said.

She compared our lives to a circle. When you first experience a loss, the loss cuts deeply into your circle. Most of your circle is consumed with *grief and adjustment*; only a small slice is occupied by *survival*.

In the second circle, grief and readjustment take up only half; survival takes up the other half.

In the third circle, survival still occupies half, but now *life enhancement* takes a slice away from grief and readjustment.

In the fourth and final circle, grief and readjustment has exchanged places with life enhancement. Now grief occupies only one small slice of the circle.

"But," cautioned Marie, "that slice will *alway* remain. Usually survival and life enhancement will control your life, but you must acknowledge and remember that grief will always be part of your life."

Our assignment after that first evening together was simple but difficult. We were to do three things: (1) Think, think, think, and remember the person who had died. (2) Cry, cry, cry, as we remembered how things had been when that person was alive. (3) Write, write, write our feelings as we remembered. In writing we would externalize our memories and feelings but, more importantly, we would immortalize them, too.

At the second meeting many people expressed inability to record their thoughts. "Give yourself time," Marie said, graciously. "It might still be too difficult to face. In time, as you're ready, you'll be able to."

To understand our responses to our most current loss, we were to construct a *loss history*. In it, we would record all the losses we had experienced in our lives, as well as our age and response at the time. Did we cry and express our grief openly? Were we given opportunities to grieve? Were we told to be strong?

This was an enlightening exercise to me. Though I was well acquainted with deaths (I recalled accompanying my parents to many funerals), I had never been taught how to grieve. I witnessed tears and sadness at the funeral home and the church service. I heard the assurance that the deceased was now in heaven. But that was all. There was never discussion about how people felt inside, only silence. And so I came to understand that grief should be felt and worked through silently, inwardly.

When my dog died, I cried into the pillow at night, remembering all the bad things I had done to him. When a classmate in elementary school died, I felt enormous grief and sadness for the family. I wept at his funeral and, later that summer, kept seeing him in crowds of children. *There's Norman*, I would think. But it wasn't. After witnessing an uncle's funeral, I had nightmares of his jumping out of his coffin.

In high school when my young science teacher died, I viewed his emaciated body and nearly went hysterical. "It's not really him, it's not really him," my friend kept repeating, until I composed myself enough to join the choir. *Never*, I told myself, as I voiced the words to the hymns, *never will I view another corpse again*. Nor would I cry in public. Future grief would only dwell within, where no one would need to assure me that corpses are shells.

A lull in my history, at least in having to attend funerals. An uncle died in Russia, a faceless name, my father's brother. I observed my father's grief from a distance; neither of us mentioned it. Another uncle died, in Germany; he committed suicide. Again, a faceless name but still my mother's brother.

Then Walter's grandfather died. Thankfully, we now lived far away in Winnipeg and I was spared intimacy with that event. Eighteen months later my grandmother died. This time I wasn't spared. I had come home for my sister's wedding, which was now followed by a funeral.

Somehow, though, this death was accompanied by less fear. Why? I don't know. Perhaps my becoming a parent and experiencing a birth had opened a door. As Grandma lay dying in the hospital, I sat at her bedside for an entire night. Her body was wasted, her once thick hair now a wire-thin braid. Her sunken face pointed toward the ceiling. Her body twisted and curled, searching for comfort. She didn't look at me.

I took her hand. "Oma," I said, "it's Elsie." She withdrew her hand and groaned.

I wet her lips with water from the cup nearby, then walked to the nurses' station. "Do you think she knows I'm there?" I asked.

"Oh yes, I'm sure she does," replied the nurse.

I went back. I sat there all night, waiting for death to take her from her prison of pain. She died two days later.

At the funeral, I couldn't look at her, even though a few days earlier I had spoken to and touched her. I knew she wasn't in that box. My fear prevented one last look. I assumed it must be a relief for my mother and her siblings to see her go. It was, but I wasn't prepared to see them grieve so deeply. *Why the pain?*, I thought, not allowing myself to feel anything beyond relief that she was released from her fiery pain.

A year later my father-in-law died. He was 59. No one was prepared for his sudden death. We flew in from Winnipeg, stayed a week, then returned. Grief accompanied us to his funeral, but I refused to pack it for our return to Winnipeg. Fifteen hundred miles kept grief and me apart.

It worked, but not for long. Four months later we moved back. Empty chairs, an abandoned truck, a too-quiet yard and house—all screamed his absence. I often thought of things to tell him, but then remembered—he's dead. He'll never know my children. I watched in silence as Walt's mother grappled with her widowhood.

Another string of deaths. A forty-five-year-old man in our church. Then a young boy of only seven. Then another, this one only five. And then Walt's grand-mother. Why is it that the old are always so much easier to bury? Again, as with my own grandmother, I visited Oma Bergen as she traveled toward death. I found her sitting on the edge of her bed, clinging to her meal tray, where a bar of soap and washcloth lay atop a kidney basin.

"I'm supposed to wash myself. The nurse left this for me," she said, pointing at the soap. She looked ex-hausted.

"Do you want me to help?" I asked. She nodded.

Together we entered the washroom beside her bed. Together we washed her ninety-year-old body. It was a holy place, that room, a shrine I had been invited to enter with her. It was an honor to help this woman who had a history of crisis and survival. She, who had walked this earth for almost a century, allowed me to do this humble task. I felt loved, accepted, yet unworthy.

She died a few days later. I visited her one last time at the funeral home. She looked beautiful. Even the cancer hadn't taken away her beauty. I no longer feared the dead. I had touched her while she was leaving. This was a right death—a long, meaningful life, a circle of family and friends nearby to say farewell, then a gentle passing.

Nine months of respite. Then John. Again I was un-prepared. Again I cloaked myself in silence. Grief Recovery unlocked the silence. "You must walk *through* the pain, not around it." Marie advised, cajoled, and drew us out—relentlessly. It worked. At least for me.

"You must learn to say good-bye to the relationship but not the memories," she told us, at the third session. Then you must reinvest that energy you once poured into the deceased person—into other things and rela-tionships."

There comes a point in a car rally—usually the midpoint—when the participant feels tremendous urgency. You want to rush, to give up finding a particular clue, and go on to the next checkpoint.

Grief Recovery was like that. I returned home from the third session, exhausted. "How was it?" Walt asked.

I could utter only one word. "Hard." Then I went to bed. All the horrible details accompanying John's death came floating to the surface. I couldn't sleep. My mind became a broken record—replaying the death, the news, all my "if onlys," and my guilt. I wanted to run.

Fortunately, the program considered such responses and provided cathartic exercises. My assignment for this week was to list my strengths and weaknesses. Then I was to list three short-term and three long-term goals for using my strengths. Finally, I was to think of creative ways to convert my weaknesses into strengths. And I was to do one nice thing for myself that week to symbolize that *I am special.*

That exercise empowered me. I could see light beyond the darkness of my grief. I could see forgiveness. John would hold no grudge for all the times I failed him. He would forgive me and so too must I. I began seeing places I could go to reinvest my energy. I could see hope. There could be meaning even with a void. It depended where you looked.

"I'm going to finish my book," I reported to the group the following week. I hadn't written a word for seven months.

"And now we have to say good-bye," Marie said, as we began our fourth session. She drew an analogy of friends moving away. At first you write often, then only at Christmas, then not at all. Eventually you make new friends. But you always remember the ones who moved away. It's a gradual process, but it has to happen. You can't live only in the past without also losing the future.

Now we were given a hard task. We were to visit the rooms and places where our memories lived. And we were to say good-bye to the possibility of experiencing that person in those settings again. "Say good-bye to the relationship, *not* the memories," Marie emphasized, as she dismissed us.

I couldn't do it, not then. But I did later. I stood outside on the driveway late one rainy night and wept into the darkness. *Never, never, will I hear the sound of John's VW coming down this street. Never, never, will I see his car zoom in, see him jump out, see my boys running out to meet him, see them all come in the house together. Good-bye, good-bye to the John on my driveway.*

I went through my whole house. To the living room, the kitchen, the playroom, the office, even the bathroom. There were countless memories residing in each room, sitting on chairs and couches, lying on the floor and the bed, even in the shower. As I said my good-byes, I realized that it was the relationship I was saying good-bye to, not the memories. I was saying good-bye to my older brother, the one who teased me, advised me, loved me.

Then I said good-bye to my children's uncle. Good-bye to Uncle John, who tucked my boys in bed and whispered silly stories in their ears and called them "turkey-lips." Good-bye to the Uncle John who tickled them, brought them stickers and snakes, and fed them Christmas decorations from his tree. Good-bye to the Uncle John who played guitar for them and sang funny songs about peanut butter, and let them strum his guitar, while he fingered the chords.

And good-bye, good-bye to the sky. No airplane shall ever buzz my house again, at least not one with John in the cockpit. No need to elicit any more promises about safe flights for my children. No more sleep-overs. No more visits to Uncle John's house. *Daniel and Matthew will never forget you, John, and Rachel will never know your face and arms.*

I did it all. I let go but, oh, I clung to all those memories. Those can never be erased, those I will always address. Those are things no one can coax and prod loose from my tight fingers. *Good-bye, good-bye, dear, dear John.*

The fifth and final session ended as the first. With tears. Tears washed away the barriers between our group. Tears knit us together in grief. For the first time I shared my poetry. "This," I said, "is a symbol of my letting go. I'll exhale my grief with these words." We wept together, not so much with pain, but with understanding.

I shall never forget those people. They deserve books in which to tell their stories. Grief is awful, yes, but it dissolves our human differences. It connects us in a way that we were meant to connect—a holy, naked way. When we turn our insides out, we're all the same. Each of us is made with the same parts. It's only on the outside where our differences show. Only on the outside do our differences divide.

Part of the healing power of Grief Recovery lies in this human connection. Initially Marie asked us, "What makes grief so difficult?"

One answer repeated itself: the feeling of aloneness. Grief Recovery meets that need. In coming together we *are* together. No longer need we mourn in silence and solitude. With the support of others we can rise again and face the pain. We can go through and not around it.

Would I recommend Grief Recovery? Yes, yes. In our last session, we watched a video about grief in which the narrator compared our feelings to a stream. Grief not aired, he said, will clog the stream, causing all emotions to be dammed up behind it. Grief Recovery helped my feelings flow out naturally.

I can't help but think of another analogy, one related to baking. Some recipes call for margarine to be added at room temperature. Sometimes I cheat. I try to add this ingredient when it's too cold. Then I'm left with lumpy dough. The fat doesn't blend into the other ingredients. Other times I try to speed the process by "nuking" the margarine. If I leave it in the microwave too long, it becomes liquid. Then it's hard to cream the sugar into it as the recipe instructs. In either case, it's better to follow the instructions.

Grief Recovery thaws your emotions so they can all play their part. In airing one's grief by walking through the pain, one gives space for other emotions to surface, too—compassion, love, and eventually joy and peace. All these emotions are suppressed behind the grief when it is bottled up.

Grief Recovery doesn't lessen the pain of grief. At times, it heightens the pain. But it helps you understand what you're going through and what you may work toward. It's like prenatal classes. They don't take away the pain of childbirth, but they help you understand what's happening to your body. That understanding lets hope replace fear, and with hope comes courage to face the pain.

Would I have healed without Grief Recovery? No doubt. But I wish I could have participated sooner. It could have helped me feel normal. It wasn't until I participated in the program that I finally knew my feelings of disassociation were normal for someone grieving. There were other physical symptoms—sleeplessness, speech impediment, forgetfulness, irritability. These were all things I had experienced but not understood.

Grief recovery isn't complete in five weeks. Some may not experience any significant healing during those five weeks. However, the knowledge you receive there goes with you. Today I still draw on things I learned there and on relationships formed there.

It was there, in that circle of strangers, that I realized how God visits us through people, even people who don't claim faith in God. It was there I met Hazel, a woman I'll never forget. "You are a picture of hope," I wrote, when the sessions were over. "You are a picture of God."

She was. Here was a woman with a lifelong history of suffering. Married at fifteen, to a man later diagnosed as schizophrenic, she put up with years of abuse before she left him. He then kidnapped their baby. For a year she didn't know their whereabouts. When she located them, she gained custody of the baby and their older son.

Hazel survived and went on to love again. Her second husband was good to her and her two sons. Then the accident. While a passenger in a car driven by a close friend (who never apologized), Hazel's husband was critically injured. Doctors told her there was no hope. If he lived, he'd be a "vegetable."

Refusing to believe this, Hazel loved him back to life. "All his bad parts were gone; only the good remained," she told me. Nine years later, just as he was preparing to return to the work force, Hazel's husband shot himself.

But that's not all. While caring for her sick husband, Hazel also made regular visits to the nursing home, where her mother lived. Her mother had suffered permanent brain damage in a fall down a flight of stairs. Hazel's friend died of leukemia. "And there's more," she said, but she didn't tell me.

Still she laughed. Still she had hope. She inspired and empowered me. If Hazel could go on, then so could I and all the others in that room. No one's story could match hers.

In that room, with all those strangers, I found meaning in these words: "Blessed are those who mourn, for they will be comforted" (Matthew 5:4, NIV). It was there, in that roomful of tears and pain, that the arms of God reached round us all. It was a paradox, for as we heaped our stories on each other's shoulders there was added heaviness, but there was also a lightening, which I can only say was God's.

How could we take away the pain of fifteen gruesome deaths? We couldn't. Only God could redeem our losses. Only God could carve a smile on all those tear-lined faces. And only God could plant a seed of hope in that garden of despair.

As we closed our final session, we formed a circle. Our hands reached out and joined our neighbors'. Then we prayed. For strength. For courage. For hope. One last embrace, and we parted.

16
Dancing with God

I'm afraid to finish this book. I've invested so much time and emotion—now where will I direct my energy? And so many thoughts and feelings remain unshared.

Today, as I sat pondering how to conclude (it is 25 months to the day since John's death), I realized how much better I feel. Every month brings new healing. That feels good, yet also a bit frightening. In the back of my mind I keep wondering who will be next.

John's death also spelled the death of my innocence. I had known death before, but not so intimately. I had always hoped it wouldn't come this close.

"I feel as though a curtain has been ripped away from my face," I recently shared with a friend. "John's death and all the other losses we experienced in 1987 forced me, against my will, to face the facts of life." Life should *not* be this way. Life, as God originally planned it, as told in Genesis 1, was "good." But today we live in a fallen and falling state, a world in which people's decisions contribute to the ongoing cycle of life and death besetting a distorted world.

That realization has been difficult for me. Before John's death I said all of us are born into the garden of Eden. "Each of us," I told my English literature class, when we studied *Paradise Lost*, "is Adam and Eve; therefore, we each can chose our destiny."

I was wrong. Not in saying that we are all Adam and Eve, but in failing to remember that originally there was only one of each. Now there are millions of Adams and Eves, and each one's choices affect the others.

With John's death, I had to accept that previous generations have hurled this generation out of the Garden. Even if I choose life-giving ways, others may not. No one makes choices in a vacuum. And so on March 15, 1987, that dark and cloudy Sunday night, Cain and Abel's story repeated itself once more.

Where does that leave me? What choices do I have left if others, by their decisions, can determine my destiny? Victor Frankl, a survivor of the Holocaust, said, "The last of human freedoms is choice." I believe that.

With my loss of innocence came this realization: I can still choose how I will live. When overwhelmed by what I see, now that my veil is ripped away, I cling to that thought. What I see, I see now through the window I have chosen. Others may have ripped the veil away from my face, but I can still choose my own perspective.

I love Kenneth Carawray's words: "There is no box made by God nor us but that the sides can be flattened out and the top blown off to make a dance floor on which to celebrate life." Through the window I have chosen, I have seen some wonderful things. The world is *not* the same without John, but I have found a whole new world to celebrate in.

Take last week. I met with Tracey, a student at the local Bible college, whose best friend had been killed in a car accident six weeks earlier. Tracey, still deeply mourning her friend, was lonely. She felt that others had completed their grief and were getting on with life. She wasn't. For an hour we exchanged stories.

"What would Erin want you to do?" I asked.

She was silent a moment, then answered, "I think she'd want me to go on."

I turned the question around and asked, "If you had died, what would you want Erin to do?"

"I'd want her to go on," she replied.

"But," I asked next, "wouldn't you want her to cry and miss you longer than six weeks? I mean, if you were friends for nearly twenty years and she could carry on without you after only six weeks of mourning, then how much did you really mean to her? How much of an impact did your life actually have?"

Tracey's brown eyes grew large; I could see relief in them. "Yes. I think you're right."

I've asked that question often when my feelings of missing John crowd out all else. If my life is worth anything, shouldn't people grieve more than six weeks? Not to be selfish, but I hope my life affects at least one person enough that he or she would miss me always. I wouldn't want someone to drown in grief for me, but I would want someone to remember the life I lived.

That meeting with Tracey taught me something important. Some of us have the gift of remembering; some of us are keepers of the dead. I don't mean this in a morbid way; I mean that we are keepers of the good in the lives of people who have died. Isn't that what the Bible is, a keeper of memories of God's interactions with humankind?

Just before this past Christmas my father asked if I planned to put something on John's grave this year. "Why?" I asked.

"Well, last year you put on the decorated branches, so

I assumed that you'd do the same this year."

I knew then that I had been assigned to be my brother's keeper. I'm one of the few who visit my brother's grave. And as far as I know, I'm the only one writing a book about John. It is a gift to be assigned this task.

"Am I my brother's keeper?" has echoed through the ages; this time the answer is "Yes!" I'm humbled by this gift. Death, seeming almost to compensate me for what it took away, has left me, not empty-handed, but holding a precious gift—the gift of remembering. Someone has to do it, for it is our only hope of finding our way back to Eden. If we forget, then we repeat. And in repeating there is only more death, more pain.

In Jewish tradition there are many well-defined tasks of mourning. One is to recite the Kaddish, a prayer of respect for the dead. It's a praise of God and dedication of one's self to the perfecting of the world. Reciting the Kaddish is a public declaration of the mourner's intention to carry on the ideals of the lost one. In other words, it is a prayer of remembrance. And in the remembering, there is a reminder of the good in all of us and incentive to work toward more good.

We need to share our own stories and hear others' stories. John's death stole my innocence but unearthed a new gift. I don't know if what I told Tracey helped her, but our exchange of stories helped me. This, too, is a gift John's death gave me, this speaking to others in grief. But again it's a gift I received only by choosing, chosing especially to be vulnerable and open about my pain.

Several months ago, within one week, three people came to me with their grief stories. All said the same thing: "I don't know why I'm telling you this. I didn't come for that reason."

I don't know why either, but I'm grateful for the gift. I'm grateful because when people share their pain with me and allow me to reciprocate, it gives meaning to John's death. In a vacuum, John's death would be meaningless. But as a window into this new world I have chosen to enter, it has become meaningful.

I learned another thing from that visit with Tracey. During our conversation she shared her struggle with the "God question." She believed God existed but was having difficulty relating to God. When Tracey was in high school, a classmate died. Tracey then asked God never to take her best friend, Erin. Six weeks ago, God had "taken" Erin. How could such a God be loving?

I felt overwhelmed with sadness. I didn't know how to answer. I couldn't even tell her that God's presence and comfort were manifested through people, because she had just said no one cared. "They say to pray for the family, but what about close friends like me?" she asked.

"Tracey," I said, "what would make you feel that God was hearing you, that God cared?"

"If God would take away all the hurt right now and make everything the way it was before," she answered.

"But could God do that?" I asked.

"I don't know," she said.

Several days later, I responded to her comment. "If there is no hurt, there can be no healing," I wrote, "just as there can be no light without darkness, no loss without love. Without the opposites, everything would be sameness. Wouldn't that be boring?"

I think it would be boring. I tire quickly of sameness; I can't imagine a world in which feelings remain unchanged. I go through feelings like a child through diapers. That's not easy. And often I berate myself for the mood swings. But I've come to accept that if I didn't get so angry or depressed, I also wouldn't feel so elated and joyful. All my feelings run deeply, not only my "weak" ones. No, I can't imagine a world without hurt. Such a world would also be devoid of passion.

God, I think, is passionate. I think Christ exemplified God's passion when, as a twelve-year-old in the synagogue, he showed passionate curiosity. Later, the sinfulness of using the temple for profit made his passionate anger boiled. In the garden of Gethsemane, he sweat. And on the cross, he screamed.

Like Tracey, Christ asked to have the hurt removed. God answered. Not with removal of pain but through the wordless message: *Remove the hurt and remove the love.* Christ on the cross was racked with pain. But in that moment, God's passion was revealed. God refused to take Christ's cross away precisely because God *is* a passionate God, a committed God, even when wounded by our rejection. John 3:16 promises that "God so loved the world that he gave his one and only son. . . ."

When Tracey and others like her hurt so deeply, they mirror God. Like God, they're wounded lovers. It's because they loved so deeply that they hurt so deeply. Death, by taking away their loved one, has wounded them. But by remembering the person despite the hurt the memories bring, they mirror God's remembering humanity despite the hurt humanity's rejection brings God.

Jürgen Moltmann, a German theologian, says, "God weeps with us so that we can one day laugh with him." We are, the Bible tells us repeatedly, created in the image of God. God is passionate, and so are we.

I long to have John back, but I don't think I'd like things to be the way they were before. My forced journey through passion has made me a different person. Would I be this way had John not died? Since John's death I feel more vulnerable *and* feel much more deeply.

John's death has taught me much about life and love and all that really matters. But it is only because I've chosen to look through a particular window, and that has taken time. I expect two years from now I'll look back on the words I wrote today and smile. I expect by then I'll have seen much more. Shakespeare said, "How poor are they who have not patience! What wound did ever heal but by degrees?"

When I began writing my wound was deep. Now it's scarring. Scars don't hurt forever but some remain more sensitive than the skin around them. John's death has left such a scar. It may fade in time and not be visible to others; I may even forget it at times. But eventually it will remind me. An unexpected blow to such a scar is painful; it's better to remember that it's there.

This book is my reminder, my constant call to look back while I strain forward. Nietzsche said, "You must carry the chaos within in you . . . to give birth to the dancing star." My chaos is John's life and death. My chaos sometimes plunged me into stormy waters, but I held on, clinging to the belief that the shore I was swimming toward would be higher ground.

Was it worth it? I often wondered: Should I fight when all I wanted was to succumb? Should I laugh when all I felt were tears? Should I love again if I could lose again? Should I believe when all I had were questions?

Still I swam and kicked toward shore. And I was right to hope, for when my feet touched ground, I danced, the star within me freed from grief and pain. I spun round and round and round. Chaos was still there, but now its pull was too weak to suck me down or spit me out.

Chaos stands silent now, a backdrop to my steps. Now I rest in the arms of God. God: my parent, midwife, and now my choreographer and dancing partner.

Since I began this book with an invitation for any who

chose to walk with me through this journey, I'll conclude with another invitation. Death, I've often said, is
difficult. But it's not unique to any of us. All of us *will*
experience death in our lifetime. How deeply we swim
into the waters of grief is a choice each of us must make.

I'm an ordinary person. I could make my world small.
By that I mean that I could always find legitimate excuses not to grow. But I think I have no excuse—not my
three active children, not my lack of formal education,
not anything. Had I used such excuses to restrict and
limit my grief, I would be bitter now. My scars would
never fade; my wounds would only scab and fester, scab
and fester.

Why do I say these things? So others may feel that
they, too, can walk the path I did. Frederick Buechner,
an American novelist and preacher said, "My assumption
is that the story of any one of us is in some measure the
story of us all."

My story, I'm sure, contains a raft of borrowed elements. I didn't write this book to parade my story. It has
been too difficult to live inside these words to merely
toss them out as food for a starving ego. I once read that
a good writer bleeds onto the pages. That is how this
book was written. I have bled, and bled, and bled some
more. Now the book is finished. I always thought I'd feel
elation. Instead, I'm tired.

I have written all these pages, and my brother is still
dead. And I still miss him. As I was writing, I sometimes
shared bits with others. Their responses always surprised me, especially the tears. *I evoked this in you?* I
thought. And then a gift. The love and comfort I
received made every drop of blood worthwhile. John's
death was not in vain. It tapped a waterfall of love.

■ ■ ■

I have a picture in my mind. It's a picture I'm looking at from high above, yet paradoxically I am part of it. There is large body of water. In the center is a piece of land. At the top of the picture is the word *shallow*. Here the water is very still.

At the bottom is the word *chaos*. Here the water is stormy. The wind whips the water into huge waves, which dance in a frenzy atop a huddle of bodies. The people wear no life preservers; still they float, clinging together, their hands linked star-shaped across a board-like figure which lies, face down, in the center.

I'm astounded as I watch, for the figure never lifts its head to take a breath. It must, I think, be either dead or not human. Perhaps it really is a board; perhaps my vantage point is not allowing me to see reality. I watch some more, then see the human craft wash up on shore.

They lie there for awhile, then slowly stagger to their feet. The first one to his feet, I note with much amazement, is the one who lay in the center. He rises in one swift motion, brushes off his long white robe, then reaches down to help the others.

I move closer, marveling at the whiteness of the skin. I expect the skin to be wrinkled. It isn't. But I see thick red scars on both his hands. Four scars he has, one on each outer and inner hand. He winces each time a swimmer takes his hand. Still he helps them up, each one.

And then the music. From every corner of the land comes music so divine I can't describe it. And then this man takes the people inside his arms and dances with them. They dance and dance until the sun goes down, the only sounds the music and the waves.

When darkness falls, the weary swimmers lie upon the sand and fall into a sleep. The man looks down at them. Then he leaves, walking right into the sea and swimming into the stormy dark once more.

The others sleep till dawn. "Where has he gone?" they ask each other as they awake.

They look around, but there is nothing there, no imprint on the sand where he slept. Only footprints leading to the sea. A look of wonder crosses each face. "I can't go back into that storm," says one. "I think I have to," says another.

The group who just the night before had bonded in their grief now spread apart. Two walk down the way the footprints lead. The others cross the land to waters which are calm and warm. No tumult here, no savage waves, just endless miles of smooth dark velvet.

They swim and swim and swim as far from chaos as they can. No grief or pain to mar their journeys here. But neither do they see an island up ahead, and when they turned to look at what they leave behind, that island, too, is gone. No dancing stars are born again, no hands with scars are ever touched again. Distance is their ally now, not love.

And the other two? They swim, face down, toward another group of swimmers. And like the one who saved their lives, they too become a buoy for others. Their chaos never leaves them but each trip ashore gives birth to yet another star.

■　■　■

If this book, my dancing star, helps someone ashore, then I shall find strength to swim out once more in waters labeled *chaos*. I don't swim well when I'm alone, but when I clasp the hand of others I can go for miles.

My brother feared the water, but he always swam. For me to choose the shallow waters would betray John. We must swim deep, we must *live* deep, and we must sing into the darkness, for dancing stars are only seen at night. Come dance with me.

Then I saw a new heaven and a new earth, for the first heaven and the first earth had passed away, and there was no longer any sea. I saw the Holy City, the new Jerusalem, coming down out of heaven from God, prepared as a bride beautifully dressed for her husband. And I heard a loud voice from the throne saying, "Now the dwelling of God is with men, and he will live with them. They will be his people, and God himself will be with them and be their God. He will wipe every tear from their eyes. There will be no more death or mourning or crying or pain, for the old order of things has passed away (Revelation 21:1-4, NIV).

Art by John Klassen

Bibliography

Augsburger, David. *The Freedom of Forgiveness*. Chicago: Moody Press, 1970.

Bane, Donald J., et al. *Death and Ministry: Pastoral Care of the Dying and the Bereaved*. New York: Seabury Press, 1975.

Bombeck, Erma. *I Want to Grow Hair, I Want to Grow Up, I Want to Go to Boise: Children Surviving Cancer*. New York: Harper & Row, 1989.

Davidson, Glen W. *Understanding Mourning: A Guide for Those Who Grieve*. Minneapolis: Augsburg Publishing House, 1984.

Donnelly, Katherine Fair. *Recovering from the Loss of a Sibling*. New York: Dodd, Mead, & Co., 1988.

Dykstra, Robert. *She Never Said Goodbye: One Man's Journey Through Grief*. Minneapolis: Augsburg Publishing House, 1989.

Hansel, Tim. *You Gotta Keep Dancin'*. Elgin, Ill.: David C. Cook, 1984.

Hostetler, Helen M. *A Time to Love* (When AIDS takes a son, a friend.) Scottdale, Pa.: Herald Press, 1989.

Kruckeberg, Carol. *What Was Good About Today?* Seattle: Madrona Publishers, 1984.

Kushner, Harold S. *When Bad Things Happen to Good People*. New York: Schocken Books, 1981.

Lewis, C.S. *A Grief Observed*. Toronto: Bantam Books, 1961.

Linn, Dennis, and Matthew Linn. *Healing Life's Hurts: Healing Memories Through Five Stages of Forgiveness*. New York: Paulist Press, 1978.

Loder, Ted. *Guerrillas of Grace: Prayers for the Battle*. San Diego: LuraMedia, 1984.

Miller, Jolanda. *You Can Become Whole Again: A Guide to Healing for Christians in Grief*. Atlanta: John Knox Press, 1981.

Nouwen, Henri. *The Wounded Healer: Ministry in Contemporary Society*. New York: Doubleday, 1979.

O'Connor, Elizabeth. *Cry Pain, Cry Hope: Thresholds to Purpose and Creativity*. Waco, Texas: Word Books, 1987.

Poetker, Audrey. *I Sing for My Dead in German*. Winnipeg: Turnstone Press, 1986.

Schmitt, Abraham. *Dialogue with Death*. Waco, Texas: Word Books, 1976.

——————————— *Turn Again to Life: Growing Through Grief*. Scottdale, Pa.: Herald Press, 1987.

Schiff, Harriet. *Living Through Mourning: Finding Comfort and Hope When a Loved One Has Died*. New York: Penguin Books, 1986.

——————————— *The Bereaved Parent*. New York: Penguin Books, 1978.

Stearns, Ann. *Living Through A Personal Crisis*. Chicago: Thomas More, 1984.

——————————— *Coming Back*. New York: Ballantine Books, 1988.

Vanauken, Sheldon. *A Severe Mercy*. New York: Harper and Row, 1987.

Wolterstorff, Nicholas. *Lament for a Son*. Grand Rapids, Mich.: Eerdmans, 1987.

Yancey, Philip. *Disappointment with God: Questions Nobody Asks Aloud*. Grand Rapids, Mich.: Zondervan, 1988.

The Author

A life truly fashioned after Christ is paradoxical. To die in order to live, to give in order to receive, to be weak in order to be strong—these are difficult truths to accept and live. But this is the Christian's call. It was with these thoughts in mind that Elsie K. Neufeld began her journey through grief following the death of her brother John in March, 1987.

The fifth of seven children, Elsie was raised like many other Mennonite children in southwestern British Columbia. Her life revolved around school, church, and farm chores. Elsie managed to sandwich countless hours reading in between these activities. Books were and continue to be her ticket to the world beyond her home.

Now the mother of three exuberant children, Elsie finds writing cathartic. She regularly visits the local bookstore. Her current loves are poetry and short novels. Favorite authors include William Wordsworth, John Donne, Gerard Manley Hopkins, Madeleine L'Engle, Luci Shaw, Walter Wangerin, and several fledgling Canadian Mennonite authors.

Elsie's faith journey began in a traditional Mennonite way, but at age eighteen she entered a spiritual desert which she didn't fully leave until 1985, when her faith finally became real. It was then that God's promise to accept her just as she was, as a human being, not a saint, healed and energized her.

This faith experience and the launching of her writing career happened almost simultaneously. Writing gave her wings, fueling and sparking her spiritual flight. The Bible, especially the Old Testament's many stories of God's faithfulness, became the fertile soil grounding her new faith roots.

Elsie's church involvements have included teaching adult Sunday school, directing a group study of spirituality and prayer, leading worship, and speaking.

Though Clearbrook, British Columbia, Canada, has been her home for many years, between 1978 and 1983 Elsie lived in Sweden, Vancouver, B.C., and Winnipeg, Manitoba. She currently lives with her family in Clearbrook, where she attends Emmanuel Mennonite Church.